Over the Edge

*"If I have learned nothing else in this life I have learned one thing;
life is nothing if not change"*

Single again after the end of a very long marriage and let me be the first one to tell you that being single after a long period of comfortable 'togetherness' can be intimidating. It doesn't hit you right away either; there are too many other things going on at first. Ultimately when you swim up out of the chaos, take a deep breath and look around, you realize there are certain... benefits that are no longer waiting just beyond the bedroom door. Ignore it for a while but sooner or later the subject demands your attention.

Twinges of loneliness set in. The desire for affection becomes an aching need. How does one meet eligible singles?

Bars are out – for meeting people anyway. That belongs to the twenties and (maybe) thirties crowd and I had been there and done that. I did go to a bar once recently with my daughter and quickly decided I was right on that score.

What to do about this; that was the question of the day. Never mind the other nagging question in the back of my brain. You know... the one that says "Well, what do you really want?"

I didn't know the answer to that one. I only knew the answer to the question what I did not want. That one was easy. I didn't want anything because I didn't really know what I wanted. I wanted time to think about it I suppose.

Yet I am still human with all the natural instincts inherent to our species and that includes the instinct to be intimately close to another human being. That absence was not going to work long-term; I had to get out and start dating. The question was did I remember how? How had dating changed since the last time I was out there?

As it turns out it has changed a lot and new alternatives abound today. Technology, communications and the internet is accelerating at incredible speed and you can now reach out and touch someone you might have never met, all from the comfort of your home and without stepping out the door. Internet dating is booming and sites like AmericanSingles.com boast membership profiles in the millions. That's a lot of singles.

After long consideration I decided to post a profile. You have to have recent pictures (raises the response rate they say), digital of course and you want to look your best so by the time you have pictures you are happy with, you have shot the evening and haven't written a word of your profile. And writing the profile itself is a trip. You have to write about *you* so now what do you say? You're back to that damn question "What do I really want anyway?"

4

You manage. Out of curiosity you start a search for eligible singles in your area that meet your parameters. It is amazing. Instantly you are overwhelmed with profiles by the hundreds; electronic mating at the press of a button. How efficient is that? For someone with no time it sounds like a dream. Guess again. It can be unexpected. It can open doors you never knew existed.

This story is about just such an adventure.

Somehow I came across AFF.com. By now I was fairly proficient in writing profiles but this one daunted me. This site is all about being open about your sexuality. I read many profiles in an attempt to decide what it was I was specifically looking for and how much I should disclose. I decided to be totally honest, especially with myself. There were things out there sexually that had recently caught my attention and intrigued me. An awakening if you will, that may have never happened if I had remained married.

I remember a few years ago a gentleman I knew suggested I was a natural submissive. This was an extremely intelligent and perceptive man and in the span of a few short meetings he saw something in me I didn't realize. Something I was denying. He was shocked that I didn't recognize it for what was. A seed was planted and my analytical mind started asking questions. What the hell is a submissive anyway and what did I know about it? Nothing, but the thought sat in the back of my mind for two years when I came across Ann Rice's *Beauty* series. It is Adult fantasy; exquisitely written Adult fantasy about submission, bondage and domination.

There is absolutely no denying I was turned on by that series and I started to think my friend had something there. I needed to find out more and I needed to explore why I was so excited by it. I took a giant leap of faith in the anonymity of the Internet and I wrote in my desires to be submissive, my fantasies of being dominated and of experimental sex. I thought perhaps if I just *said* what I was looking for, I might find it. My handle is Miselena and this is where it began.

Miselena

I am very fit and slim and expect my sex partners to be at about the same fitness level. I dislike the bar scene. I prefer privacy and discretion when I'm involved in sexual encounters. I like my partners to tell me what to do in the bedroom. I tend to like experimental sex and enjoy anal sex. I'm almost always willing to try some light bondage or blindfolds. I am not interested in married/attached men who are lying to their wives/girlfriends, men going through a divorce, men under the age of 38, or couples where the woman is being pressured to participate; I don't respond to e-mails or profiles that have no face picture or are simply crude. I prefer men that are at least 6 1/2- 7 inches, shaven or closely trimmed (this is a must), and healthy (no heavy drinkers, STD free please). I will provide you with my face pictures once I see yours. I expect kindness, courtesy and respect in addition to pleasure. Finally and most importantly: if you hold women to a double standard when it comes to sex, if you throw around the terms "slut" and "whore", or if you only view sex as something that men "take" and that women "give," we are most definitely not a match.

Looking For: A man or couple (man and woman) for Erotic Chat, Email or Bondage & Discipline

Ideal Person: He is confident in his masculinity, adventurous... sensuous, strong, commanding, playful, affectionate... confident, smart and not afraid to give direction. Understands the power of suggestion... and knows how to turn up the heat; discretion is imperative.

And so it began…

October 25

Hi Miss,

I am 6' tall, 195 muscular and fit. I am told I am attractive and I have to admit looking at your pictures and reading your profile you exude submission and light bondage but as you suggested you seem to enjoy the power of strong suggestion and coercion over strong verbal direction; in any event you are extremely attractive and your fondness for anal sex is very pleasing. Anyway I know you said if there is no picture on the profile beware (yes I can read), but this once please your curiosity and contact me, you may be pleasantly surprised!

October 26

Hello, I am a friend from AFF that sent you an email without a picture...You graciously (probably more curiosity than grace, but I'll take either one) accepted my email and requested a picture... Here is my picture; I hope you are "pleasantly surprised". Please understand I am seeking friends so I want to be up front with that, I am not searching for the love of my life, I enjoy exploring and exciting the mind and taking intimacy to higher levels with lots, and lots of teasing, playing and experimenting. As I suggested I enjoy a bit of domination where I am in control and I can see the obvious excitement and anticipation of a willing but directed partner... if that is not you, I appreciate our brief meeting at the site. Oh, I also wanted to say I am currently out of the states on business travel and will return soon (which if it turns out you are interested will give us a chance to communicate), so if you are looking for an immediate encounter (which my first observation says you are not) I can not accommodate that. I hope you enjoy the picture!

October 26

Hello D,

Thank you for the picture; I have attached a facial picture of myself for you. It would be nice to see your face if you are so inclined...
I appreciate your candor regarding relationships and certainly understand where you stand. I am intrigued with your comments regarding submission / domination and would like to explore that further with you. This is a relatively new self-discovery and I am curious to see where it will lead.
I hope your travels go well and look forward to hearing from you again,

~Miselena

October 27

Pleased to meet you Miselena. After seeing your picture, I am definitely inclined (to send another picture that is) you are an attractive woman and even your curiosity excites me. I think in each correspondence I've read from you (this includes your ad) there is a sense of wanting to know so much about the lifestyle but an apprehension that some "nut" will go too far. Let me put you at ease (or at least the best I can do from afar) nothing should ever happen in this area unless you have some trust of the individual that you are experimenting with. I have had a few experiences in this area, (only a couple long term due to the nature of my work and some other influences, but usually our fun stopped because either I moved or my partner moved) in each case my partner felt completely safe, we were both careful to probe limitations going only as far as we were BOTH felt comfortable. Now you might say how can you be in control if you only go as far as your partner feels comfortable, and I have two responses to that: first, you begin by setting initial limits to learn about each other's bodies, personalities, desires, fantasies etc... etc... etc... and as you become comfortable, each person's natural tendencies will come out (believe me it won't take long)... my natural tendency is dominant; it appears that your natural tendency may be submissive, I believe this is what you wish to find out.

Second, let me worry about the control or suggestive part (I am good at it ha, ha, ha). If you truly have a submissive nature we (you and I) will bring it out. One other thing I have found that works best if you are new to this - it is sometimes better to have "sessions" of play. I once had a friend (she) said that it was hard in her normal relationship to go to the limits that she was truly curious about so she appreciated our "sessions" because she would have been embarrassed to initiate or suggest the things she wanted in a normal relationship. I am not suggesting that you have similar feelings or desires; I am only saying some people feel more comfortable with the thought of having this outside of a normal situation so they don't feel uncomfortable around their normal partner. In fact during some sessions there isn't even penetrating sex but I don't want to let the cat out of the bag.

So let me ask Miselena, have you ever experimented in this area before? What has your curiosity peaked so? Have you fantasized of submitting to your partner, what is your role in these fantasies? Oh I almost forgot I have to tell you if this goes anywhere I always, always, always wear a condom and practice safe sex, I am not making any assumptions with you but believe it or not some people want only skin to skin and I just want to bring that out up front. I also gathered from your ad that you had a bit of a concern about respect; know this, there will never be a problem with me disrespecting you. Contrary to belief complete disrespect and dominance/control are not necessarily synonymous. Make no mistake - with a firm grasp, a strong deep tone, my whispers in your ear and the knowledge that I have your mind and body - this will be enough to get us started; where we finish will depend on where your mind takes us! Are you still interested?

October 27

Hello D,

You write extremely articulate letters and I am now more curious than before to see what will become of this correspondence. You are correct on many counts and that shows a perception I hadn't expected. I find myself exploring my limits these days and I think that has been generated from the fact that I'm pushing my limits at work right now (in a totally constructive way) but it has opened the door to my wanting to push limits in other areas. I *am* apprehensive about the partner I choose to explore this with and have had some limited experience with one other person. I appreciate you wanting to assure me that I would be safe with you and thank you for taking the time to do so. As far as being submissive, I already know that I am and that it is something I need to find more out about myself. I have a highly responsible position at work and am the sole support of my family and the attraction to submissiveness is the release I'm finding I need to leave control behind and in the hands of another. I will willingly let you worry about the control.

Of fantasies, I have many and I am always submissive in them. Your comment of a firm hand, deep tone, whispers in my ear and control of my mind and body excited me very much... and yes... I am more interested than ever. I look forward to hearing from you again D,

~Miselena

October 27

Hello Miselena,

Thank you for your gracious compliments on my writing. I am glad to see I have added to your curiosity regarding your submissive tendencies. Hopefully, we will both find pleasure in your curiosity. You mentioned my perceptiveness, which I also appreciate but I think it's a requirement, how else could we explore the limits we sometimes bind ourselves by. I absolutely have to be conscious and aware of your reaction to everything we do so we will know when to take the next step as we lay a path to your satisfaction and ultimate release.

When I read your letter immediately I knew (or at least I think I know) that sometimes with the weight of our day to day responsibilities, chores, etc... we are depended on by so many people to come through and make decisions. In some instances the decisions determine the success of others, in some instances they can even determine life or death (in the case of nurses and doctors). In any event we all have to have some form of release and believe me it is an awesome feeling to have somewhere, or sometime where you are not in control, where there are no decisions to be made, where you only have to listen and react and obey whatever direction you are given. Along those same lines and even deeper somewhere, where you trust that your every movement or thought is not judged by the norm but only by the moment.

I once had a friend that said after a "session" she would just pass out... the complete feeling of release was just that intense for her, and the fact that she didn't have to look at me and say *did we really do that*, but only enjoy the experience for what it was and to look forward to the next adventure, even anticipating the next session trying to figure out what I might come up with next caused us both quite a bit of excitement.

The exploration that you want to have in this area I think is very normal, many people have these thoughts, and desires; not many have the courage to explore them. You have to ask yourself are you capable of taking direction explicitly (in the right setting of course), some people do have a problem being comfortable with releasing control. During a session you might be told how to prepare yourself, what to wear or not to wear. What to say or not to say, held by strong hands and told to masturbate but not allowed to climax until the time is absolutely right or determined, and just when you wish to speak, have fingers pressed gently across your lips commanding silence. Are you capable, and does this even excite you? As I said, in reality it is not all about sex, it is the control and submission that is intoxicating.

Have you ever wondered/fantasized about what it would be like have your body on complete display for another, completely giving yourself up to your partner? In my mind our first encounter would be very vanilla coffee or lunch of some sort. However the second encounter (and I have no doubt there would be a second) would begin our sessions, and I would tease you and control you from the very beginning, very subtle acts to get you wet and excited but control nonetheless, and with each session or event I would increase until ultimately you are completely mine (during these sessions). One thing I do enjoy, I love the sight of a collar on a beautiful woman, especially one with a slender sexy neck such as yours; it sets the tone for the session and allows you to get directly into the mood.

Now I have a few questions for you, to help me gauge your desires, during the times when you mentioned you experimented with light bondage, were ropes used, chains, and restraints? Did it excite you? Is that you in the picture with candle wax on your breast? I once knew a woman that would absolutely climax at the feeling of cold steel running across her nipples or clit, I think it was a danger thing for her but the feeling would always send her over the edge... Does the thought of someone talking dirty to you (within limits) excite you or do you take it simply as being vulgar? Have you played/experimented with toys, and finally have your fantasies ever included double penetration (anal and vaginal)?   Now let's practice; when you reply, type into the first line "for your pleasure"

October 27

Good morning D,

I find that your letters are as exciting and arousing as any I have read and hope that my response elicits the same feeling for you, for your pleasure is as important to me as is my own. Indeed, I believe that the gift of giving pleasure far exceeds the reception in terms of satisfaction. And as to whether I was being gracious... I think not... simply observant. The compliments are true in fact and I do not give them lightly.

You have once again expended considerable effort to ensure I feel comfortable and safe. This is a comfort to me, as I suspect you know, and appreciate that you are determined to do so. It again shows great perception and intelligence. You ask a great many questions in this letter and I will do my best to answer them with all openness and candor for if we are to go down this path, I wish to do so with brutal honesty – to you, but especially to myself.

Am I capable of taking direction and releasing control; I believe I am. I do currently in my work environment in many areas but those instances are brief and once direction is given, I am free to carry out the command as I see fit. I know that this does not apply to that of which we speak; however it is indicative of the ability to take direction. The total direction of which we speak is what entices me for I will not be required to think beyond the request, but simply to comply with it.

Have I ever wondered/fantasized about what it would be like have my body on complete display for another; yes, but in my fantasies I am blindfolded and therefore anonymous... or so it feels. Giving myself up completely; absolutely and have done so before.

The restraints I have experienced were very nicely padded, thick leather wrist restraints, and yes, watching them put on me as well as how they looked on my wrists excited me very much.

That *is* me in the picture with the candle wax; indeed, it is me in all the pictures I have posted and sent to you directly.

Dirty talk... hmmm.... There is such a fine line there for me. I mostly think it is vulgar; however, if done with taste and the intent to arouse with suggestion, I find it can be stimulating. Personal preference in this area is difficult to describe and the boundaries between what I believe to be tasteful or vulgar, even more so.

Toys... oh yes, I have played with them often and double penetration has entered both my fantasies and real life – albeit with one person and toys, never two men. Have I fantasized about being with two men... yes.

So there you are D, the bare and honest truth. Now, if it pleases you... tell me how you feel...

~Miselena

October 28

Miselena,

I was very pleased with your last letter; it was very well written. Also very good on your "for my pleasure" response, as you suggested this is absolutely for our pleasure and so I will modify the statement to "for our pleasure", include this in each of your responses to me!

It is absolutely important that you are comfortable with whomever you take this journey with, so you are correct it is important for me, because I want to take you to the limits that you only fantasized about. I want you to do things (of your own free will) that you thought you could never do. When I say "your own free will" this is what I mean; there will be a time when we are face to face where I will ask that you step forward if you wish to be tested, if you want to explore, but if you do you lose all control (we will of course always have a safe word that will stop any play if you are truly uncomfortable). During these times you will be told what to wear or given what to wear.

So where do I start. I admit I am absolutely stimulated by the thoughts of a potential encounter with you. I am excited at the thought of sharing something special that many people only dream about in the corners of their mind but never share. Excited by the thoughts of opening our minds to things that may be new to both of us, as each time experiences/limits are different. Each experience has its own life and none are quite the same. I am excited at the thought of seeing your first orgasm while collared for me. I see your mind as a canvas, a fresh painting and the scenes we create, any explosions we share will absolutely be originals because they will be from you. I have to remind you my business travel will have me out of the states for a bit (possibly two months) I hope that this does not discourage you.

You questioned whether I was as excited or pleased as you with our correspondence thus far. I have to say I am absolutely pleased with the direct way in which you have responded. It is very important that we are absolutely clear with each other. I will certainly be clear when/if we become physical and clear in the direction that is absolutely necessary in a Sub/Dom relationship. It will always start off with the collar (mood). Sometimes candles (I love, love, love hot wax, I enjoy the look of anticipation waiting for the next piece of wax to drop and dance on the skin).

You mentioned restraints, my goodness what an incredible turn-on to see a woman restrained or blindfolded and completely submissive and restrained. You also mentioned several fantasies. Including double penetration, very, very hot! A fantasy that many submissive shares is the fantasy to be the center of attention. The center of a couple of men or many men; in other words they are blindfolded and kept in the presence of their partner who is in complete control, then displayed, touched, caressed, and fondled by many men while their partner gives them direction and guidance, the partner keeps them safe and the situation under control and the sub pleases (without sexual intimacy) the men present.

For some that is too intense, for others just the thought makes them wet. That is a powerful fantasy especially when blindfolded and the sub is unable to determine how many are actually there, like I said very, very powerful. Me I like the thought of your hands tied above your head with your breast well exposed, your legs spread far apart, blindfolded and listening to my voice as I tell you what you will do. It is in that type of scenario that talk is so important, so powerful to whisper in the submissive's ear giving a detailed description of how she appears, how sexy and sensual she looks and what is and what will be expected. Talk that is explicit but not necessarily dirty or vulgar describing your full breasts, your eager private area and the satisfaction that both will have if direction is properly followed can be powerfully intoxicating. It is in this position that nipple play can send you over the edge. To be worked up until the desire to be filled and satisfied overcomes all else; it is here that you will completely submit. It is here that your limits will be tested. Now touch yourself and tell me in your next email if any of this makes you wet?

By the way Miselena have your ever been spanked or fantasized about it?

October 28

Good morning D,

I hope this finds you having an amazing day... I find that it takes considerable time and thought to do justice to your correspondences. I am enjoying them so and perhaps even more than reading them, responding to them. It pleases me greatly that you are pleased with my letters and as you may suspect, encourages me to match effort for effort.

I find what you write to me and how you phrase your thoughts is erotic in the extreme. They make my breath catch and heart pound and yes, most certainly arouse me in the most pleasant manner. That you desire me to trust you so implicitly that we may, for our pleasure, push our limits to the edge is positively exhilarating. That you are so clear and concise in your expectations... is intoxicating. I look forward to the time when we are face to face.

I find your anticipation of our potential meeting delightful. That you seem to be as excited as I, I believe portends great things. You have twice now mentioned collars... I have done some reading on the subject (among other things, I am a research analyst) and am intrigued by this. This would be an entirely new experience...

Am I discouraged by the length of time you are out of the states? Perhaps. I suppose we shall see as our correspondence continues to develop.

Regarding multiples... again something that would be entirely new and you are correct in that it would require my ability to trust in you completely. I like the idea of your whispering in my ear while blindfolded... certainly one of the most vivid of my imaginings. And nipple play... yes, you are an erotic man. You cannot imagine (or perhaps you can) what this does to me.

I have complied with your request, although it was not necessary to touch myself to determine I was wet... that truth was evident before I made it half way through your letter. And spanking... yes...and I found I enjoyed it very much indeed. It is, in fact, one of the areas I wish to test my limits.

I am looking forward to your next letter D, and hope you continue to enjoy mine.

~Miselena

October 29

Miselena what field do you work in? Just a curiosity of mine.

I hope that this letter finds you and yours safe, and secure. As I watch CNN I see the devastation that is going on back there, and I am still amazed.

I must say thank you, I am very pleased with our correspondence thus far. You have been everything I expected, and I trust that this will blossom into a unique arrangement of mutual satisfaction. Each time I read a letter from you I am stimulated by the anticipation of what is to come. I think we are driven the same. Our roles so clear our passion so strong. You the submissive and me the Dominant! I request and you comply. No thoughts, no judgments, only complete obedience; are you willing?

I received your last email, I am glad that it takes some thought to reply to my emails; I want you careful and sure that you really are ready. I have to tell you, you are truly better at this than you think, I suspect this has been something you've struggled with for some time; perhaps something you did not quite understand or attempted to suppress. Not to worry, we will definitely release what you have inside. Step by step we will test your limits in many, many ways. I have to smile a bit though because I can already sense your desire, your desire to submit and drift into my commands. But remember this, I will take advantage of this, not in a negative or abusive sense (I am not into abuse or humiliation) I will direct you to do things (during our sessions) that you would not ordinarily do, and I will take pleasure in your compliance.

We will both see that you too will take great pleasure in your ability to please and to be pleased, to exceed what you once thought were your limits, and relish in your ability to overcome previous boundaries, set new heights; but make no mistake Miselena, during our sessions my requests will be followed implicitly. You will always prepare yourself per my direction, sometimes I will tell you what to expect, and most times I won't. Do you like surprises Miselena (again only what we are both comfortable with).

As for the trust this goes both ways; I will trust that you know yourself, and that if you are truly uncomfortable you will use whatever word we deem as the 'safe word', but keep in mind once used it will stop all play! No harm no foul but we will stop for that session. This will eventually encourage you to seek your absolute limits. "Should I use my 'safe word' or can I take just a little more?" All the while your body will be begging and needing to explode. I am often so excited by this dilemma and believe me Miselena you will be too! So we will trust and respect each other...

Apparel/Toys: In my minds eye your collar will be leather, about 1-1.5" inches in thickness (thin and feminine), large silver studs (distinct not gaudy) with a D-ring in the center. There will be toys, and we will have our favorites, some very, very large, some small and delicate. The large ones you will try to take and we both know you will not be able to, but I will enjoy seeing you stretched and filled. I will whisper over and over my pleasure at your efforts to please, and discipline appropriately any half-hearted efforts.

One thing in your letter that stood out, well ok, there were a couple of things. I am glad you share my fondness for spankings, but keep in mind spankings do not only occur on the rear; a well placed gentle slap on your labia or clitoris could send shivers through your body in the right mood. Even spankings while bent over and exposed/open can excite both your rear and your front and create extreme wet pleasure, this is one of my favorite positions especially if shaved or well trimmed! I can explore and taste extensively in this position, and it lets me discover your anal limits. It is the mix of pleasure and very, very light pain that makes this so sensual; we will determine together your level of tolerance for this. Or perhaps you already know? Tell me.

I am also very pleased to hear how nipple play stimulates you. You do appear to have perfect breasts. Have you ever had soft clamps on your nipples? They restrict the blood flow to the tips of your nipples, once removed the blood rushes back to the tips making the nerves extremely sensitive, some have the same sensation when placed carefully on the labia.

Since you are an analyst, have you ever come across pictures that truly excite you, intrigue you, and stimulate you? Especially the ones that you were embarrassed by yet compelled to save, or analyze perhaps even masturbate to late at night when you are deep in thought and alone. It would please me if you were to forward me a picture like this (and briefly what excites you about the picture). A picture that embarrasses yet excites you. Now tell me when was the last time you pleased yourself and perhaps I will share one of my experiences, but only if you ask me properly.
"for our pleasure"

October 29

Good evening D,

I must say I look forward to your letters with such anticipation and tonight I had to laugh with delight... even your subject line brought a smile to my face.

Thank you for your concerns about my and my family's welfare. We are faced with a horrendous situation that grows more awful by the day. It has been a totally surreal experience... smoke as thick as the thickest fog I have ever seen and snowing ashes. I feel such empathy for those less fortunate and we have many employees that have been affected grievously. Today was better here than the last few days and the troubles have shifted east of us, much I am sure to the dismay of many more families. I am well and safe as is my family. I hope any relations you may have here are safe as well.

I was startled by something you wrote… that I am everything you expected. That you had expectations from my profile or from subsequent correspondences? If it pleases you, I would like to know what those expectations were from the start; I am comfortable that I begin to understand what they may be now. I believe there is no doubt, in your mind or in my own that I am submissive by nature and you suspect correctly that it is indeed something I have not only struggled with but have attempted to suppress for years. It is sometimes a difficult thing to reconcile with the role I play in life and in the support of my family. My sisters would argue that I am the strongest among them for they only see the outside and have no concept of what lies within.

I absolutely loved how you wrote of my desire to submit and drift into your commands; your words are so powerful and I am again amazed... I will take your admonishment to remember your mastery of the situation seriously as it is for our pleasure we begin this exercise in the first place. I believe you will find I will always seek to comply with your wishes.

Do I like surprises… really D I had to laugh; have you ever met a woman who doesn't? Perhaps you have but I am not among them; I love surprises. And I appreciate the additional discourse on trust and respect. That you so clearly define the rules of play demonstrates your respect and trustworthiness most eloquently.

On the subject of apparel and toys; I find that the idea of wearing your collar quickens my senses and arouses me in a way I have not experienced before. Truly, just reading your words has an astounding effect on me physically. I cannot begin to imagine how intense it will be should we ever actually touch and I so long to be able to do so. Do I know my limits or tolerance level? No, I do not, but I have no doubt that you could take me there.

Thank you for the compliments on my breasts; I am fortunate and blessed in my looks and have done nothing to earn them other than attempt to keep them in good standing, but I thank you all the same. Clamps; I have only experienced clamps on one occasion, very briefly and enjoyed it very much. I am so looking forward to the play you mention and even now throb in anticipation.

I am afraid I must disappoint you on the subject of pictures. Have I ever come across any pictures that excite me… without question. Any that embarrassed me but felt compelled to keep… never. As well, I never masturbate to pictures. My imagination is sufficiently vivid that I have never needed such props and being a visual person, perhaps you can begin to understand the true effect of your words on my imagination. It is positively explosive. I admit that I read and re-read your letters many times.

The last time I pleased myself was yesterday and will undoubtedly do so again tonight as soon as I post this letter off to you. It would please me greatly if you would share one of your experiences with me, if it also pleases you to do so.

Good night for now D; I wait in anticipation of your response.

October 30

Miselena,

I am glad that you look forward to my letters, I do so look forward to yours as well, they really do please me. I am also glad to hear that your family is in no danger. I could hardly believe it. Your schedule will be just fine if we choose to continue this. We both speak of being discouraged (with reference to my absence), but I am very confident that

14

you will wait. I sincerely believe there is something in this for both of us. That leads me to your next comment. You are everything I expected with regards to finding someone that is attractive (and you certainly are as I have already mentioned), yet open and eager to explore things that are not the social norm.

I expect you to be able to let go and accept your desires. You certainly seem ready, willing and capable of doing just that. I expect you to see past the norm, and to explore to a greater depth, areas considered taboo; anal sex, submissiveness, light bondage, light discipline, exhibitionism, toys etc... Even to speak to these issues on a fantasy level is far past what many consider normal. Frankly that is what I enjoy about myself as I alluded to; you dream and seek what many will not allow themselves to admit. You seek release and that is why I am so confident I can give you exactly what you seek and in turn you fulfill my urges to dominate; it is a symbiotic relationship; one of mutual satisfaction and gratification. That is why you meet my expectations.

As I said if we are to get the most out of this you must be able to unload; eventually you will shed the day's stresses like layers of clothes and you will stand before me naked, unable to do anything but comply with my wishes and satisfy both our desires!

You did not find a picture so how will you make this up to me? I will accept a suitable substitute picture. How will you please me?

You asked (correctly) for one of my experiences, I will share this one with you. Keep in mind I will not do this often, later it will be your role, part of our excitement to determine if these are experiences of mine or future experiences you will have (with me of course). In any event I would hate to ruin a potential surprise for you.

***

This session began with a phone call at work. "Prepare yourself; I will arrive at 4:00". Her preparation involves a bath using only scented soap (I am a very clean person and love the scent of fresh soap), and a fresh trim/shave. I knock on the door and it swings open, she is behind the door completely naked except for the heels. I step in carrying my bag. The door shuts behind me, and she stands before me head lowered in anticipation of her collar. She is eager to begin; it has been a long day. I hesitate intentionally prolonging the moment. I gently lift her chin with my finger looking into her eyes. "Are you ready" she only nods. I place the collar around her neck, and begin sniffing her sweet soft skin. First her neck then shoulders, circling her breast. I tell her "you are very pleasing to me" she says "thank you", she understands that during these times she is to be silent and so I can only assume that she is in need of a spanking.

She immediately turns around and bends over the chair. I only speak one word, "ten". Slap, 1, she counts. Slap, 2, she counts enjoying the feeling of my hand bare against her behind stinging but in a pleasurable way. She counts to 10 without loosing count; she knows that if she looses count I start over. On the final slap she turns and we continue, but first I look into her eyes to ensure she is ready to proceed. I reach into my bag and remove a set of wrist restraints, a set of weighted clamps, and a large dildo made of wax and a long rope. I stand the dildo on end and light it with a match. I place the wrist restraints on her wrist and tie the ropes in place. There is an eyebolt installed in the ceiling; I run the end of the rope through the eyebolt and gently pull her arms above her head to secure her firmly, but without pain.

I take the padded clamps and attach them to each side of her meaty vagina, the small ball weight attached to the clamps pull her lips naturally open and her mouth gasp with the weight securely in place. I pull her hair back while taking the dildo candle off the table and whisper, "you will now see why it is so important to follow my instructions implicitly". "Open your legs wide". She complies immediately sensing what I am about to do. The dildo is huge and she is not certain she can take it, I continue pulling her head back by her silky hair, I place the candle between her legs and she can feel the heat of the candle on her inner thighs, this warmth seems to excite her incredibly, "Do not close your legs." She nods with understanding.

Slowly I slide the dildo between her wet lips the flame is getting closer and closer to her clitoris. Once it is deep inside her I instruct her to use her muscles to secure it inside, again she nods. I remove the clamps from her vagina and attach them to her breast one to each nipple; she is now moaning from the heat of the candle and the pressure on her nipples, I can tell the weight is an incredible added turn-on. With one hand I have a firm grasp of her hair, I pull and whisper, telling her how beautiful she is, how wet she is and how eager her vagina is to take this huge toy deep inside, while whispering I run my silky tongue into her ear and slide the toy inside her in a penetrating motion. Her moans are quite audible, she is ready to explode, between the heat of the candle between her legs and the weight of the clamp on her nipples she begs me with her eyes to let her complete her release.

"You may speak" I say and I move from her ear to her eager lips, passionately kissing her, intentionally blocking her speech, pulling her hair and penetrating her wet vagina with the burning candle. She begs vocally, "please can I"? My first response is always no and I stop. She tells me what she is suppose to, "I am yours for direction and obedience" I smile and continue until…

***

Wow… Five days into an email correspondence and I was hooked. This man was speaking to my most secret desires and stroking every nerve along the way. I couldn't wait to get home and see if another email had arrived. The pleasure I derived from reading and responding to these emails was so intense I often wondered if reality could live up to my imagination.

I was determined to continue on this journey, anxious to see where it would lead. The emails were becoming more demanding, placing expectations upon me to fulfill requests. The transition from simple correspondence to accepting direction was as smooth as to not cause the slightest ripple of doubt that I was safe and from here it continued on along the same vein for quite some time.

October 30

Good morning D,

I am gratified that you look forward to my letters as well and that they please you. The anticipation we are building with each correspondence for the express intent of our pleasure is positively delicious.

Thank you again for your compliments and explaining your expectations. I believe I will live up to them and you are correct in your assertions that I am ready, willing and able. Your confidence that I will wait is well founded, in both theory and fact as reality offers no alternative.

I did disappoint you on the picture issue and you ask how I will make it up to you. I need some additional direction in what exactly it is that you wish from me. Do you want me to find a picture that meets the requirements of embarrassing but compelling? Do you want additional pictures of me? If I can engineer it, would you like pictures of me with another (this might be tricky), if so, a man or a woman? I am not procrastinating; I simply wish to comply with your expectations and to please you with my efforts.

Thank you for sharing one of your experiences with me; I am pleased that you chose to do so and that you felt that I had earned the right to hear it. The picture you sent was astonishing and the subject a truly beautiful woman. It is perhaps a bit more than I have envisioned for myself but then this is all about pushing limits and I will abide your direction as you see fit.

Have a wonderful day D; I will be back in touch tomorrow,

~Miselena

October 31

Good morning Miselena,

It is always pleasing to see a letter from you in the morning. I enjoy this immensely! Very astute of you Miselena, I am disappointed with the picture, however, this is a minor infraction, nonetheless there has to be consequence so, I would like two pictures. First fulfill the original request. Find an embarrassing yet compelling picture the guidance is a picture of a submissive female (collared) in an embarrassing yet compelling position! Second provide a reality picture of you. In your picture I want to see you penetrated both anally and vaginally (a toy will suffice so no outside participants are necessary, this time)! I was inclined to have you get a picture of you with another, my preference would be a man, however; since I still require the initial picture we will explore multiple participation at a later time, which may include a woman. While we are on the subject do your fantasies ever include women? Again at a later date I will request a picture of you with another man, but this will be later!

Once I participated in an event where a woman was the center of attention. She stood naked and blindfolded (this event was at her request), there was no sex involved but she was touched, caressed by both hands and lips. She took direction and complied without hesitation. She claimed to have climaxed several times. It was in a very private setting, and very exclusive of course. It was an extremely erotic situation, but to ensure success it has to be very private, discreet, all participants have to be mature, respectful and clean.

This leads me to another subject. Some confuse erotic and just plain nasty. The two are not the same and should not be confused. We will explore the erotic! If you so desire we will stretch your imagination and your physical limits. You will please me in many ways and I provide you the compete release you require. I will be very direct and firm but not vulgar in any way or abusive.

Now I would like to know if you have ever had the company of a black man...
A woman?
What is your normal sexual preference?

November 1

Miselena I trust you had an enjoyable trip or at least bearable...I will bend my usual rule this time and write a little something for you to ponder through your weekend. I have given your question about expectations a bit of thought. It was indeed a great question! I enjoy being sexually dominant, I enjoy thoughts of control and challenging others to see past what is in front of them. I enjoy administering spankings and other erotic pleasures until the person is past the brink of where they thought their limits were. When it's over the pleasure is so incredible and the thoughts so intense that you relive them in your mind over and over.

I want to challenge you, and if things work out I will challenge you to do things that you may have only fantasized about. We will share things that you may not have had the courage to do alone. Things that a real boyfriend or partner might not ever do or once done might question/judge the outcome. It is unique to say the least but it is also incredible!

You mentioned once before that you thought I had an erotic mind. Absolutely! I would even go so far as to say I have a dirty mind ha, but I am educated, experienced and mature enough to translate those thoughts into something incredibly sensual. I will have no hesitation in giving you clear guidance as to what I expect; I will tell you the how, when and where, and you will come to understand that your immediate compliance, without hesitation is essential.

We will get there. That is something we will build to through trust and understanding. So far I think the chemistry is right, and I readily admit that I am somewhat turned on by thought that this is somewhat new to you, and perhaps you are even a bit frightened by the thoughts you have, and ultimately giving yourself completely (if only for short periods) to someone else, following directions, and relishing in the fact that you are so capable of submitting so easily. I am extremely patient and firm, and together we will immerse ourselves in the roles we will assume creating erotic images that we will replay over and over in each other's minds. Ultimate discretion is required because this is for us and us alone; if I send compromising pictures of others they will be completely unidentifiable or if I take or request pictures of you they are only for me. I expect the same.

When you return, I want you to write your expectations! Keep in mind your role in this new found "relationship" (respect)... This could be as simple as a single sentence if your desire is only to be submissive in the casual/general sense (example taking simple instructions, directions etc... during sessions) , or it could be more elaborate if your desire is to push limits with clamps, multiples, etc... Although I have to remind you that anything we do either simple or elaborate will 1. Be legal and 2. Be safe. Perhaps a fantasy of yours is in order at this point. Yes I think that would be nice. Describe to me a fantasy, be as explicit as you like!

My goodness isn't this fun. I hope you enjoyed your weekend.

November 1

Good morning D,

Imagine my surprise and pleasure to see two emails from you! I will attempt to do justice to them both. There are some absolutely lovely thoughts expressed within and there is something very compelling about the way you write. I hope this finds you well... where ever you are.

18

We are back to the subject of pictures and I have included not one, but two pictures I found compelling. Both are startling and I think the composition extremely well done but one epitomizes the phrase "pushing your limits". Not that I want to push myself so far mind you, but because these were artistic as well as erotic. And I completely understand that the pictures are for our pleasure exclusively. Your second request would require the purchase of toys I neither have nor have any wish to have around my home; it would please me greatly if you would reconsider. Please do not misunderstand me. I will not hesitate in following your direction during a session. But I have no wish to allow this into other areas of my life, and my home (or homes) are a part of that. In one I have children and the other provides a different sort of refuge that I need in my life. It would feel an intrusion and I hope you understand. Should I find myself in that particular situation and can avail myself of a camera, I will take advantage of the opportunity and send you your pictures; I simply cannot predict the timing of the issue.

Have my fantasies ever included women? Yes and in life as well. If the situation is right I am inclined to enjoy couples but my natural preference is with a man. And yes, I have been with a black man. You also know that this is relatively new and my experience very limited. I believe this compounds exponentially the physical sensations I have when I let my imagination drift as you suggest.

My expectations... some are very defined and some still fuzzy. I expect kindness, affection, humor, closeness, sensuality, that you are commanding, firm, erotic, intuitive. Things I already believe you to be. My desires are to submit all control to someone I can trust implicitly. Someone who will not only help me learn more about myself and my limits, but will direct the effort as I am certainly neither capable nor qualified.

Fantasy? Hmm...

***

I am restrained, arms forward in wide, padded wrist cuffs that dwarf my wrists, bent over a counter so high I'm on the tips of my toes. There is soft candle lighting, exotic music and you... whispering in my ear as you direct me through the steps. My legs are spread very wide and I am being spanked; there is a dildo in my rear and occasional slaps nudge this deeper. My hair is being held tightly making my neck arch back. Sometimes I have a second person in the scene performing cunnilingus, sometimes not; I think I would like it though. Once I am pink and flushed, you turn me over, sitting me up with my legs wide and bent at the knee, feet flat on the ground. Again you tug firmly on my hair pulling my head back but also keeping my hair out of the way of the candle you now have. Slowly the wax tips and falls on my breasts making me gasp. You love the way it looks... I love the way it feels. You decide that clamps are in order and you gently suck my nipples into your mouth once they are in place, moving down my body until you are centered on my clit with tantalizingly long, slow, rough strokes. I have let go and can do nothing but feel...

~Miselena

November 3

Well Miselena good day to you as well... We had a bit of a storm a couple of days ago but the weather is beautiful today. I know in some ways I am very fortunate, the job I have has me traveling all through Europe. The pictures you sent were very, very nice... Oh heck they were awesome... It is apparent that you do enjoy nipple play as much as I. They remind me of a very, very erotic scene, I will elaborate on this later in this letter.

It is amusing that you chose the pictures that you did, I am quite familiar with the clamps and weights that are used in the second photo...although the ones I have used in the past don't have weights that are quite so large. None the less I really, really enjoy giving nipples plenty of attention, and I will relish in the thought of what I will do to and on yours!

I completely understand your apprehension of allowing this "pleasure" or "play" to extend beyond "controlled limits" in other words, I don't believe either of us would like for this to encroach in other areas of our lives; your thoughts regarding this actually mirror my own, this is for our pleasure only! It will remain separate from all other things. This is meant to enhance us both, to set free that which we normally contain. I have to reiterate I will immerse you in things that others only dream of; the only requirement is a willing heart. Ok, and a bit of courage as well. There will be no standard boxes allowed during our sessions... is that acceptable to you?

You mentioned that your home provides you a different type of haven, what did you mean by this? You also mentioned that you have no toys, I found that to be quite interesting. This may surprise you but I am somewhat pleased by the fact that you have no toys. I will introduce you to much, and the thought that some things may be brand new brings a big smile to my face. As for my initial request I will not reconsider; I will however be patient. I understand some of the thoughts that may be going through your mind. So far all you've seen is several emails, and a mysterious picture, but there is so much more. Once we have experienced a physical encounter (I certainly hope it leads to that), enjoyed the pleasure of thoughtless obedience, you will do as I request without compunction or hesitation (yes I know during our sessions), you will trust that my sincere concern and awareness will serve us both well.

Please do not worry; I will never put you in a situation that will jeopardize your safety or our discreet behavior. Miselena you will know the pleasure you seek and I will give it to you. I have to tell you, your email today brought a smile to my face, and yes I believe I am all the things you mentioned. So along that vein I will not reconsider, but as I have said before Miselena I am very, very patient and I will wait until you have the opportunity to provide what I have requested (remember I do not wish you to do anything that will jeopardize your privacy).

Keep in mind Miselena my patience may cost you. Remember the story where I mentioned the number 10; I have yet to decide if you will take them across your rear, or across your clit Although if I am forced to admit it, I enjoy an extensive round of cunnilingus after a nice spanking - something about tenderness after firm discipline. That all being said I realize a bit of patience is required on both our parts, so be patient for my return, and perhaps I will take the pictures I desire. So for now I wait.

That leads me to another quick thought; I mentioned earlier some things go hand and hand. I truly believe that you can not have submission/discipline/bondage without an appropriate amount of tender sensuality. You will find I am quite capable of all and in fact the sensuality accentuates all others. I think you will be quite pleased.

Now more on the nipple play I described above; I have had many erotic thoughts, and a few erotic encounters, for some reason when you mentioned your nipples it reminded me of one (yes I know I did not clarify one encounter or one thought), specifically a young lady completely naked and blindfolded in front of me, kneeling on a pillow. Her arms are free for the time being. Her legs are spread wide; I have placed weighted clamps on her labia her lips are spread, pouty and pink from the weight. Her clitoris is quite swollen and she is very excited anticipating what may come next. I place a glass of wine to her lips, gently urging her to sip.

Her lips part, her mouth opens. What a sensual site, giving to her this sip. I reach over retrieve a bottle of oil that has been warmed, and I explain to her that it would please me to know what pleases her, with that I squirt the oil over her breast, arms, stomach, clit and I suggest she run her hands over her body.

Her initial motion is too fast so it becomes evident that I must direct her actions, specifically telling her where to touch, how to touch. She is performing under my strict direction and guidance. I stand behind her whispering to her building her excitement. I can see the desire building and her hands begin to migrate to her vagina, I slap her on her rear, a sharp slap that brings immediate attention. I pull her hair reminding her that I did not direct her to touch her vagina, her strokes return to her body, focusing on her heaving breast, running lightly around her nipples. Her oil soaked hands seeming to glide over her upper body while I watch this incredibly erotic sight. I probe her soaked vagina from behind, it is wetter than I've ever felt. I nudge her forward a bit, penetrating her anally and vaginally. I can hear her gasp, and I know she is ready. She is allowed to continue, finally I whisper it is acceptable for her to finish. Immediately she moves her hands to her clit, and the ensuing explosion was incredible. It was quite a site.

Miselena, I can not over emphasize that I want this to be pleasurable for you; I will get my pleasure from seeing you explore things you've never or seldom experienced in the past. This is what excites me. My intentions are not to add stress to your life in any form but to encourage you to explore. I will be firm in my desires, but I do understand the limitations that we will deal with. Please understand that I want to stretch your reality as it appears to me that your imagination is already quite bold.

Before I go I have to mention the blacks, couples (I was even a birthday present for one wife) and females comment. I have played with all the above and the thing that peaks my curiosity is how would you react if you were the center of attention (in reality not fantasy) of another man or woman, if you were completely in the receptive mode, blindfolded while cunnilingus was performed on you or even entry with me present are you even capable of such a thing? Have you ever thought of yourself naked in front of a stranger? Have you ever visited an adult book store?

Oh this might be a good time to begin thinking of a safe word. I have words that I've used in the past but in this area I would prefer the word be something you are very, very comfortable with. They have to be words that would not come up during a normal encounter. It would be amusing to misunderstand and stop all play at the peak of your excitement, or maybe not so amusing.

Ok, one last thing really. It really has been a pleasure so far. I know many things that I suggest or mention are in contradiction to what you may have experienced in the past but I assure you if we continue, the erotic possibilities are only limited by our imaginations; I know that the things I would have you do would be things you would or could not do on your own, it is important for us both to thoroughly understand this!

I will admit I was quite pleased to see your response this morning and can't wait to see what your response will be to the things I've addressed in this email.

Write soon.

November 3

Hello D,

I hope this finds you having a lovely day. You are indeed lucky to be able to travel as you do and see and immerse yourself in other cultures. I would do much the same had I the opportunity. How are you finding the sentiment toward America these days? Interesting?

I'm pleased you enjoyed the pictures; they were certainly very compelling to my mind, and thank you for your patience on the subject of personal pictures.

It is evening now and I have the time needed to finish this letter properly and reply according to your wishes. I would have liked to write soon as you requested but Monday is reporting day and I am in charge of all that... I rather liken it to boot camp... intense and doesn't let up all day.

So back to pictures... as I re-read your letter you say it is amusing that I chose the photos I did... why do you say that? I chose them based on several criteria, that they were tasteful, artistic, arousing and compelling.... and probably in that order. I'm interested in hearing your thoughts. I'm glad you thought them awesome by the way.

You ask if I have a willing heart and the courage to live outside the box... you are a perceptive man... what do you think... you have had an opportunity to read several of my letters now and I have been very forthright.. how do you see me fitting into this so far?

I want to thank you again for your understanding and comprehension regarding your second picture request. I appreciate your patience... and certainly good things come to those who wait... or as a very dear friend of mine says, the longer you wait, the more in abundance it comes. It would be for our pleasure that this turn out to be true.

My home... yes, it is a haven and I don't allow many distractions from that. No television, no stereo, no outside influences at all. Total silence and peace. It is where I go to get away from everything and have recently broken that only for my laptop... but it is still silent here. I find it helps me unwind faster, to decompress from the day and allow me to hear myself think, for I am definitely a thinker. I have come to cherish the time I have here and have filled this space with things that belonged to or remind me of the people I love, and many I have lost. It keeps me connected and I find myself comforted by it.

So... you are somewhat pleased I have no toys... I don't know what to say to that other than I suppose your being pleased is a good thing, even if unintentional. It certainly allows you greater freedom of creativity from which we should both benefit. Why did you find it interesting? And you think I have a bold imagination? I would have to agree on that point... one of my favorite attributes actually and has always served me well. You stimulate my imagination on many levels... please feel free to continue... lol, I do so enjoy it.

Ah... what next... yes, the center of attention question. That is a very interesting question and I am not sure how I would react. At work and in most things, I am a very 'behind the scenes' type of person. I avoid being the center of attention because I don't care for being scrutinized too closely (gee, can't image the why of that). This is a bit different. It is being there yet removed in a sense. I will think on it some more. And no, I have never thought of myself naked in front of a stranger nor have I ever been in an adult book store.

22

As to safe words... perhaps that is something to save for discussion when we meet for the first time. You will be able to give me some input on that subject and I will listen carefully to your advice. I will be interested to hear your thoughts on the matter because I am not sure why the simple word 'stop' wouldn't suffice. I think myself capable of refraining from the use of that word unless I felt it was necessary but I will defer judgment until we can discuss it further.

You are pleased by my letters... can you guess how that makes me feel? I am pleased by yours as well and I hope this brings you the same sense of joy I get from your praise.

Be well and safe,

~Miselena

November 4

Good day to you Miselena,

I must say you are right, I am quite lucky. I am unbelievably fortunate to have found someone as attractive as you and even luckier someone so curious and yes willing. As far as American sentiment goes, you'll be surprised at how welcome we are around the world. Most of the countries disapproved of the war, or for that matter any war but as a whole America is well respected worldwide. It has been my experience that most places I've visited mimic the American culture; unfortunately they are beginning to mimic the bad things we do as well. Maybe we'll discuss that at length sometime when you're feeling a little philosophical.

Just a reminder, don't be so quick to thank me for my patience (the pictures) it will cost you dearly. I do so love a cherry colored rear end although I have a sneaky suspicion we'll both enjoy whatever appropriate payment I come up with. As for my comments on your choice of pictures being amusing perhaps interesting is more accurate than amusing. If I correctly assess what I have seen so far, you are a woman that enjoys proper attention to your breast, they are after all nicely proportioned. I simply found it interesting that the photos you chose focused on that part of the anatomy.

On that note it is funny how certain parts of the body solicit certain physical responses from us all. For me the breast, and believe it or not the neck are highly erotic pieces of the female anatomy they arouse me greatly in addition to a nice rear end. I think that is why the collar excites me so; it does something to accentuate the neck and I find it very arousing and stimulating. So to read your email then see the nipples, pierced and weighted it was like icing on the cake; perhaps it is the exaggeration of reality that make those types of photos erotic for me. Suffice to say we will examine this area (not the piercing of course) extensively and we will include all your erogenous zones! What about your inner thigh?

Miselena to answer your question on what I think, I know you want to play outside the box. I have no doubt that you want to experience many of the things I've described so far, and you will. Perhaps not to the extent of some of my thoughts but you will at least have a taste. I believe that once your palate is wet, you will be intoxicated by the surreal affects of what we will share, drunk with lust as it were. It is then that we will see how you "fit", and that is when I will take you past where you could go alone! I will safely encourage you to do that which you would not do on your own. We will see where your limits are. Who knows, your limits might just surprise us both. The fun thing will be finding out. Everyone is different, no two individuals are the same, and no two individuals will share the same reaction, - that is what makes this so beautiful. So where you fit, we will see, how you react we will see, and where this takes us we will see. What we know is you will be completely submissive during our encounters, you may be on your knees, you may be on your back, you may be bound, you may be blindfolded, restrained, spanked, teased penetrated anally, vaginally, toys and real – all these things!

I have been quite pleased but my expectations will grow, and you will have to grow with them.

I am impressed - you have assumed your role well; it is very appropriate that you address your request in exactly the same fashion that you have addressed me in your emails. "If you desire", "If it pleases you" etc. Even in your apprehension with the second photo asking/requesting that I reconsider; that was very, very nicely done. I will require that you continue along those lines if this is to continue.

I think you are the perfect candidate; you understand this has nothing to do with degrading or humiliating behavior but everything to do with release and exploration. Yes I am quite pleased. Now I must ask you, how do you feel when you read my letters? Yes you have said they excite you and that you get pleasure from them. I want to know in some detail (yes describe this to me in writing) how your body responds to the parts that excite you. Do your nipples swell? Are you extremely wet? Do your labia and clitoris swell? Does your mind drift and your legs open? Perhaps inviting a brief round of masturbation? I want you to touch yourself tonight. I want you squeeze your nipple for me to the point where they are on the brink of pain, then release and take them into your mouth, giving them the tender attention they need.

Imagine me between your legs, licking you gently then raising up to blind fold you. You hear a knock, and you feel me leave your side, the door opens then closes; you ask if you may speak and I answer firmly yes. You ask if you may ask what that was, and my response is don't bother yourself with that, enjoy... there is silence again... you are told to spread yourself open so that I may continue, mmm it is good, I alternate applying pressure to your clitoris with my full lips then gently suck your lips between mine... mmmm you want to explode… I whisper in your ear, "is it good" but you realize someone is still performing on you...

On a different note, it is interesting that your haven is so restricted. In other words you have done a very good job of limiting outside influences. Nice touch. Silence is a good backdrop for playing and it allows the mind to wander, and I believe acts as a stimulant to our imagination. When we play we will experiment with both. Sometimes using soft jazz as a backdrop other times dead silence, only the sound of our heavy breathing will break the silence. As far as clothing I have yet to decide what you will wear for our first encounter; I do so enjoy sheer things. Whatever it is it will be something that I choose for you. I will bring it with me, and you will disrobe and change into what I have chosen without hesitation and you will be prepared per my instructions (to be given before that encounter).

What you wear or don't wear are extremely important depending on the mood or intended setting. I think part of the sensuality of this lifestyle is the apparel; some enjoy leather, heels, spikes etc... I enjoy a softer more sensual setting, nonetheless whatever I have you wear will be classy and sensual but leave no doubt that I am in control and that you are submissive and obedient.

Ah I see I may have struck a nerve with you being the center of attention. Yes you will be the center of attention; from our first communication I sensed that you enjoy leadership from the background as opposed to the foreground that is why I will take such pleasure in thrusting you into the center, but again this will be some time down the road. In my thoughts you might be standing in the light, and in the darkness there may be me, there may be me and someone else, but you will not be able to tell who or how many. You will be asked to do things that will please me, and I will definitely show my pleasure. Now Miselena in the privacy of your home think of what you would do to please me while standing in the light... How would you make me desire you even more than I do now?

I have attached a photo; tell me does it make you gasp? Does it offend you? Does it frighten you or cause you to fantasize about your own sexuality...

Oh, one more thing I saw the wax on your nipples but have you ever had wax dripped on your pubic area?

Enjoy your evening...

November 4

Hello D,

Thank you for the compliments; you are very generous to say so many lovely things. I am glad that the sentiment toward America is healthy and respectful and it is gratifying to hear.

Once again we return to the subject of pictures... if it pleases you, let's start with those I chose. There was very specific direction I was given in regard to content, namely that the picture include a collar. While I came across many (well maybe not many... I'm fairly selective) some that were focused on other parts of the anatomy; they didn't fulfill your requirement. That is not to say you are mistaken in your assertions that I enjoy attention to my breasts for you are quite correct in that. As to the inner thigh, I can't say that I have any immediate reaction and I suppose that is because it is an area that has been sadly unattended in the past. It will be interesting to see how I feel about it.

The second picture subject revolves more around the lack of that picture. You admonish me to not thank you so quickly; I will head that advice.

And your latest photo... I suppose this photo brings up the subject of what I consider attractive versus unattractive when it comes to genitalia, and loose, hanging flesh is not attractive to me... on either men or women. When performing fellatio I prefer the testicles to be tight, all the better to stroke and tease, or at least I believe this to be true. So, did I gasp, no; was I offended, no, but neither was it erotic to my mind.

We share an attraction to the neck area D; I very much like to be kissed on the nape of my neck and it sends the most delicious shivers through my body. I would be pleased for you to do this for our pleasure as well.

You make yet another interesting comment in your last letter... that you are aware that I want to step outside the box and you believe we eventually will, but what I found interesting was the comment that perhaps I would only taste these pleasures and not to the extent of your imagination... I am most curious as to that extent and wonder if it is something about which you fantasize. I have no doubts that you will take me beyond my current experience and push me to do those very things I would never do on my own. Indeed, you already do so and if I did not think you capable and you did not think me willing, we would not continue to correspond. It will be something, this finding out.

You would like to hear of the physical effects of your letters on my body... I believe you will be pleased to discover they are many. It starts with my heartbeat and slow warmth suffusing itself outward from my chest and affects my breathing next which slows to almost nothing until I find myself taking a gasp of air. That is when the throbbing begins and I can feel the blood rushing to my genitals and swelling the area increasing sensitivity. My skin then begins to tingle and it is as if I can feel every nerve in my body electrified and on alert. Every time I take a deep breath the body rushes begin anew and make no mistake, they are full body rushes. It is most delightful and you have a capacity to bring that to me unequivocally.

How would I make you desire me more than you do now? What a lovely thing to say, that you already desire to be with me, but back to your question. I have no idea... I suppose I would touch myself in a manner that was arousing to me in the hopes that it would also arouse you but I have to admit; a big part of what I am attracted to is the ability to put myself in a position where I don't have to think. That is what I am trying to escape... I don't want to have to think; just respond. I imagine I will think about our encounters long after they are complete.

You introduce two scenarios in this last letter and they both involve other people, albeit as a future event, but already you urge me to push limits, if only in my mind, and you create a very erotic picture to assist me down that path. This leaves me in absolutely no doubt whatsoever that you know exactly what you are doing and have begun the experience we are to have already. You are using this luxury of time until we meet to its fullest advantage and it betrays your intelligence once again.

Wax... yes, but not as extensively as on my breasts. I will do as you request tonight but I have to tell you that I can neither take my breast into my mouth nor even get my tongue remotely close to the nipple. Perhaps the photos are misleading as to their size, but they are very small. Likely part of the reason they have maintained their shape despite my age. It would please me if this was not a reason for reprimand. I am after all, only capable of what can physically be accomplished.

I hope your day was lovely.

~Miselena

November 5

Good evening Miselena,

You are correct and accurate. I did specifically mention the collar and had you missed that point I would have been able to continue your tally of payment. (I think we're at 10) So you made a very astute observation which solidifies my previous comment "you will be perfect". It was nice to see that you are a neck person as well. You also responded to my question regarding your inner thighs. Rest assured there will not be one area on your body that I will not touch! Additionally, you will masturbate extensively in front of me, while I explore you in other ways.

I greatly appreciated your honest reaction to the photo that had the weights hanging from genitalia. Your perspective in this is appreciated and as with everything we will discuss and perhaps try, I will take your input under consideration. As I mentioned above I will explore every inch of your body. I will enjoy you most when your wrists are bound (with padded restraints). Sometimes your wrists will be in front of you so that you can be physically guided with minimum conversation. Sometimes they will be behind you presenting the ultimate submissive position! In each instance I will explore your body intensely while I bring you to the brink of climax, wave after wave of anticipation until you are at a point where you beg to explode! My tongue will explore areas that others have neglected and together we will discover all your buttons.

How appropriate your response regarding thought. I will neither require nor entertain your thoughts during our sessions. Your only input will be the response your body provides me. That is all I will require; the rhythm of your breath, the swell of your nipples, the sounds from your lips as you gasp and moan under my fingers, tongue and yes toys.

So what were the results of my request? Did you feel the self inflicted pressure/pain on your nipples as you teased them, imagining me in your ear directing the course of your action? Oh no dear there will be no thought required when we play. It will be the norm for you to follow my every instruction and you will come to know that the reward for such obedience is great. Yes you will recall over and over in your mind things we have done and the mere thought will make you wet. Oh, and no your actual physical limitations will be/are no cause for reprimand although I will tell you now, there will be a problem if you say "please reconsider, I think that is too big to fit in me". While we are on the subject, your breasts are ample enough to please us both!

You asked the expanse of my imagination. It is vast, there are those things that are fantasy (that will remain fantasy) there will also be those that we will bring into reality; when I say only a taste perhaps you will not be given to several men but only a couple (not including me). I have those that I know are safe and I trust implicitly. To display you in a manner that accentuates your beauty and obedience would be most pleasing. It is extremely important to me that this scene and every scene not be cheap, but a sensual experience for both of us. Very important is the who and where involved in these scenarios. Eventually it might please me to share the pleasure you give me, this is an example of "taste". I know you are willing to please, from seeing your body I believe you quite capable of pleasure but I want the level of confidence we have in each to reach a point where you can simply put your head back and absorb what is happening around you as a matter of course. You mentioned to me that trust seems very important to me. It is without question the most important thing. Without that the rest cannot properly flow!

Something that is quite interesting to me is the difference in pleasure from a man's perspective as opposed to a woman's. I have engaged in threesomes, multiple guys with one woman, even two guys and two girls (swap), however I have never participated in two women pleasing each other without my direct participation; my role as a director for lack of a better title. This is a fantasy of mine, to facilitate the pleasure of one woman (woman 1) at the hands of another woman (woman 2). To give instruction and guidance as one woman brings the other to climax after climax (because women can be so sensual, so soft) Once I am pleased that the recipient (woman 1) is properly satisfied I provide satisfaction (to woman 2) in a way that only a male can do. Swollen and thick I would enter first with vaginal penetration and then the ultimate is a reversal, the woman previously being pleased (woman 1) performs cunnilingus while I enter anally her tongue running from my scrotum and testicles to the tip of the woman's engorged clitoris. Finally feeling woman 2 climax with me inside, feeling her muscles tense and squeeze my shaft incredibly hard as wave after wave rushes over her body.

You believe your photos might be misleading? We will have the opportunity to take others; sensual and stimulating photos (very, very discreet photos) from every position, you will be my center, relax and enjoy!

Tell me Miselena just out of curiosity, are you more comfortable at night in a T-shirt and underwear or do you typically wear a nightie (teddy or such) as a rule?

Do you take pleasure in fellatio? I would have you perform this on me regularly but in a specific manner. I will teach you what pleases me in this area. Along those lines some women are quite turned on by the mere thought of having seminal fluid released on their skin, this hot fluid massaged into their skin at the point of orgasm, released over their swollen breast, and hard nipples while passionately kissing or whispering sensually in their ear. Me I most enjoy watching a woman's reaction during her own orgasm, watching her face, her body tensing writhing in pleasure and releasing as she spasms in the throws of ecstasy. I enjoy seeing her come down as she relaxes in a feeling of euphoria; it pleases me to see this before I allow my own release.

Miselena, tonight I think I would like you to go to the kitchen and retrieve a fork from your drawer. Do not remover your underwear! Close your eyes and run the fork very, very lightly over your lips from your vaginal opening to the tip of your clit, very soft and continuously; long slow stroke after long slow stroke. Describe this feeling to me. You are not required to think of anything specific; only allow yourself to drift and perform the motion I requested. Describe the feelings you experienced while doing this.

November 5

Hello D,

It is evening and my day is almost over. I am ensconced in my haven here in CA and it is blessedly quiet. Now I can relax and give my full attention to your letter before I picked up a book and read myself to sleep... oh yes, and I will do as you request as well.

You have twice now said that you think I will be perfect... I don't know if I should be flattered or scared to death by this comment but regardless of my feelings, I comprehend the need for me to 'get to the bottom' of some of my thoughts and desires so I suppose I will choose to be flattered and push aside some of my apprehensions.

I am pleased that you appreciate my honesty. I don't know if this will mean anything to you yet, but I can assure you that I will be honest in all things with you. I am with everyone actually. Don't mistake that however, for volunteering information; I am extremely circumspect in all issues. It would please me if I could expect the same in return and do indeed feel as if you have been honest in all things with me. That you will take my thoughts into consideration speaks volumes and is greatly appreciated.

'I will neither require nor entertain your thoughts during our sessions'. I think that may be the single most powerful statement you have made thus far.

The results of your request were lovely; I am so thankful I was blessed with a vivid imagination. I'm also visual and can close my eyes and create an environment, indeed... lol, I do so often with the scenes and directions in your letters. You are already providing me with an escape from the maddening world. (Maybe that's a bit to harsh, life is actually very good to me and for which I am very thankful.)

I started out with firm pressure and gradually increased this until it was as hard as I could stand; my breath shallow at first and graduating to gasps. It was not long before my heart started to pound and the familiar warmth began filling my body and flooding my labia. You were whispering in my ear and encouraging me to take more... just delicious...

You ask if I would like another taste? This put a huge smile on my face. My first reaction? I wanted to say duh...lol, but then I thought you might misinterpret that as being disrespectful and I certainly have no wish to go there. So, my official response - I so look forward to your letters and am always looking for another taste. I hope you enjoy writing them as much as I enjoy reading them for our pleasure is surely what we each seek. You certainly seem to enjoy the writing of them for they are filled with lovely detail and are varied in their themes. Their cadence is rather exquisite as well; I believe you mean it when you say your imagination is vast.

What do I wear at night? Hmmm... sometimes cotton 'booty pants' and a camisole, sometimes flannel pajama pants and a 'crop top'... tonight I'm wearing flannels, and oh, by the way... almost never wear underwear so I will have to put some *on* to comply with your request.

And yes, I enjoy fellatio and I will be pleased to follow your direction... I take great pleasure in the giving of pleasure and in fact look forward to a great many things with you.

I hope your day is lovely,

~M

November 6

Hello Miselena,

Well it is Thursday here in Europe. Although we had a beautiful week (weather) it appears we may be in for storms this weekend. I saw on CNN international that your area was hit with a bout of rain as well, hopefully not too bad. It is amazing how the news exaggerates things sometimes.

If I recall correctly this is your day to travel so as always I wish you a safe and enjoyable trip. Have you decided on your mode of travel? When last we spoke of this you were undecided between air and auto. If I have gauged you correctly you enjoy the auto because it affords you the time and opportunity to reflect on past experiences, and absorb the beauty that surrounds you. Sometimes we are so wrapped up in keeping pace on the treadmill of life that we forget there is a manual setting that will allow us to set our own pace. We often have to be reminded to enjoy that which surrounds you.

As usual if you do not receive this prior to your departure, enjoy your weekend and we will begin anew on Monday...

So tell me Miselena what were the results of our little experiment? Did you retrieve the fork as I requested? I hope I made it clear that you were to run the sharp edges over your panties. What an exciting thought; I can not wait until the night we explore the kitchen together. There are many things there that we will employ for our pleasure.

Yes Miselena I do so enjoy writing these letters and reading/sensing your responses. I utilize this time to set the stage for what is to come (you are very perceptive) and although we both seem to share an active imagination, our courage to bring to reality that which our mind creates speaks volume about our character as individuals. I am certain you have been chosen for your current position based on what others have observed in and about you. You are extremely intelligent and that excites me. It excites me because any idiot can engage in the physical motions of sex. Do not get me wrong there are times where just sex is appropriate, raw, passionate and animalistic. That is not what I would have from you however, for you I have bigger/better plans. From you I would have your mind. I want the thoughts of what I would have you do dancing as you drive along the road. I want the thoughts of what you have done playing over and over making you incredibly wet. We both seek more than just sex.

***

Today I see you in a hood, your collar firmly affixed to your neck. Your arms spread wide over your head inviting me, teasing me to take you. Your legs spread equally wide open, it is as if your body has formed a human X -your wrist and legs bound at each end. I check to ensure you are quite secure and comfortable. I don't want you thinking of anything other than the stimulus I am about to provide you. It is truly a pleasure seeing you in this position. Your body exposed to my imagination; how should we paint this canvas today? I can tell under the hood that your eyes are wide with anticipation. You are already wet and I am watching as your breasts heave steadily at a pace that is a concern to me, so deep so fast. I whisper to you, "Miselena you are in my care during these times, your safety, and your pleasure are under my control, relax and obey." Your only response is a gentle nod.

I have many toys Miselena and today I enjoy the cat. It is a whip with 12-15 fine leather strips. Your body is on fire, your nerves are on edge, you can not see what goes on outside the hood, and you can only feel as I run the cat over your body, over your nipples, your breast, your navel and between your legs incredibly slow. You feel the warmth of your excitement following my cat, like hot liquid over your body. You can sense the potential danger and that danger magnifies your excitement. Several strokes of this erotic object have your body quivering for release. I stand in front of you naked and hard. You can feel my warm breath outside your hood. You can feel the tip my penis hard and swollen as it teases your swollen clit. You know that this is more of my control. You feel my swollen penis brush over your leg, so hot so hard. "Miselena your body pleases me, you know this." Again a silent nod from you. I am still so close you can feel my hair touching your skin. I lift the bottom of your hood and you let out a soft "no"!

"Oh sweet Miselena" I say as I lift the hood only to your lips and gently, place a passionate kiss on your wet lips. My lips are so soft and you realize you have spoken during a period of silence. You feel me releasing your wrist and legs, and you wonder what is next. "Five my sweet Miselena" I whisper. Slowly I guide you to a table, where I attach your wrist and ankles to the feet of the table; you are bent over and your behind is exposed to me. I run the cat down the back of your neck, allowing the strips to tease your skin. The first swat stings and you forget to count, the second swat brings you to reality, you resound with 2, and I correct you. No my sweet, you missed the first one. you know to correct yourself before I strike again... 2, 3, 4, 5; your behind is tender now. It is a cherry red.

While still secure and exposed I slide my tongue between your wet lips sucking them gently in my mouth. You still feel the warmth of my discipline on your behind but also the gentle touch of my tongue now deep inside you; what an incredible feeling. Firm, strong, in control and command yet capable of such gentle pleasure. You are at the brink of orgasm when suddenly I stop and release you from your position. I ask that you kneel and return the pleasure I gave you, immediately you drop, I lift your hood to your mouth

30

(you still can not see) and you take me into your mouth. I am so hard and firm you feel my veins swell as you take me inside. As always I reinforce how wonderful and talented you are. You please me greatly this way and you know that this day you will climax over and over. You feel my head swell as if I am about to explode, but I take you firmly by your shoulders lifting you once again to my lips.

I have two very large toys that you will take today; one anal, one vaginal; it is good that you do not see them. I spread your legs and perform on you, bringing you to your first orgasm which is an explosion. I continue until your juices are flowing freely. You feel me probing and you know that it is incredibly large but you also know to be silent. Slowly, slowly, slowly you are filled, my goodness you feel stretched to your very limits. Again my tongue goes into action. "Miselena you must pinch your nipples for me, I desire to see them swollen and pink..." You immediately comply and this orgasm is much quicker but just as violent. You hear me whisper... "There is more". You feel me probing your rear, "relax my dear"; you are not sure if you can take this, but you know the consequences of a failed effort. I always encourage you to take more than you think you can handle but not more than that which gives us pleasure; it is incredible to know that with each accomplishment your desire to do more, give more increases. On this day we are both exhausted from satisfaction.

I will comment on your night clothes later... for now thank you for a beautiful week, I so enjoy sharing these thoughts with you. I am confident of where this will take us and I know the journey will only be half the fun.
Enjoy your weekend. Oh don't forget to tell me about the fork!
Oh and your thoughts of seminal fluids on your body.

November 8

Hello D,

I hope your weather isn't too awful this weekend and are the kind of storms that provide an extra edge of electricity to the atmosphere. We have some of the most spectacular storms in the desert. We did have some rain here and need all we can get. The entire west is in the midst of a four year drought and hopefully we will get a lot of snow this winter.
I am not traveling this week and next week I will be flying; it will be soon enough that I have to see the devastation left by the fires so you see, you are correct once again. I do enjoy the drive, and for the very reasons you suggested. I try to find the beauty in every surrounding though and don't often need to be reminded.

The results of our experiment... hmmm... I have done this particular exercise three times now... and not because I found it so thrilling the first time that I couldn't resist a bit more, but because I wanted to give it every opportunity to be what you would have liked it to be to me. Will I disappoint you if I say the sensations were merely pleasant?

Hmmm... Perhaps it will take you to show me...

'for you I have bigger/better plans; from you I would have your mind...' What a flurry of emotional reactions this statement has caused and is largely responsible for the delay in my response. You see D, you cannot have my mind unless you are also willing to take everything that comes with it and you have made your position very clear on that point. Indeed, you almost lost me on this comment for I am sorely tired of men who want my body and my mind and nothing else. It is a pattern I am determined to interrupt and would lose considerable self esteem if I allowed it to happen once again. So, having

given this considerable thought, I have decided that I don't want to walk away from this experience, but if you want my mind, you are forewarned, for I will yield to you on this only so far and to the extent I wish.

Having said that, may I discuss 'just sex'? Just sex is not at all what I expect or in fact, have experienced with you thus far. You are so correct in knowing how intelligence and mental stimulation contribute to a truly sensuous experience and I have no doubts on your mastery of this. I am constantly amazed by your letters and that you can do so (amaze me so consistently) fairly screams your intelligence, perception and creativity. You have already fulfilled so many of my expectations... indeed, I believe my ad states 'kindness, courtesy and respect in addition to pleasure' and you have been and provided all those things in abundance.

Shall I tell you how much I enjoyed your last story? It leaves me in a bit of a quandary... would I purposely speak so I might enjoy the entirety of the scene... I think I might. My anticipation of what could be, in the incredible pictures you paint... is heart-stopping. That sensation, the one when your heart is pounding and you feel like every nerve ending in your entire body is alive... is very hard to find. You have brought me here countless times already and we haven't even met. I find that astonishing and I have such wicked fantasies of you already. I would speak... no doubt about it, just to test you because I'm always pushing the envelope. You are absolutely right in that every experience encourages me to let go a little more, to give more.

You ask about semen and I don't have any strong feelings one way or the other to offer up. As far as fluids rubbed into my/your body for our pleasure... I am particularly fond of scented oils. What are you fond of? What makes your heart stop? It would please me if I could bring you the same exhilaration I feel.

You have comments on my nightclothes? I have to smile... I can't imagine what they might be and can't wait to hear them...

November 9

Miselena, today was a beautiful day... I've spent time in the desert before, in fact the Mojave and you are right - it is beautiful - the red canyons and the clear night skies and all the life. Desert life is really a contrast to what most would believe. Kind of like us.

That's a nice segue to address some of the things in your letter.

First let me say thank you for your compliments regarding my level of intelligence and perceptive abilities. You are very generous. I would like to think that I am perceptive and maintain a keen awareness of what is going on around me including my partner's needs and desires, but it is always nice to have my thoughts confirmed so thank you.

Now for our experiment; you have made an assumption here my sweet Miselena. You have assumed that the fork was to stimulate you to climax. Perhaps the experiment was to de-sensitize you to the sensation so that when I do this without panties or perhaps using other objects (that I will not mention in this letter) you are able to compare the sensation. Additionally, as you eloquently alluded to, it is the combination of multiple stimuli that will create the environment that we seek. So as a lone stimulus perhaps it was merely pleasant; however, applied with a bit more pressure, while blindfolded or hooded while I whisper to you what must be done, just perhaps the sensation may be a bit different. Or maybe I'd add a little warmth to the fork (not scalding hot) hot enough to say get your attention which leads me to another area that we've only touched on.

There will be times that you will no doubt test my conviction to have you do as I desire. It is inevitable; you know the subtle things that you will slowly comply with (remember without hesitation) or the words spoken without solicitation, or perhaps a request not fulfilled; they are meant as test for me. Your test will be met first with firm encouragement from me, then with discipline. Are you prepared? Let's discuss this for just a second. Discipline can be candle wax dripped slowly on your nipples or clitoris until the feeling of control is rinsed from your body and you desire only to submit yourself and follow whatever gentle encouragement I provide. Discipline can be spankings or whippings across your behind, across your back even across your sex. This is another area that admittedly I enjoy. Keep in mind Miselena, submission is like a gift, I am completely aware that you are giving yourself ultimately when you relinquish this control, it is the ultimate gift. That is why it is so important we completely understand one another.

I had to smile at your comment "you will yield only to the extent that you wish." I have concluded from the very beginning that this will go only as far as you are willing to allow it. We will discuss, debate, etc. many aspects of this lifestyle in a quest to understand and release your true desires and expectations but make no mistake - once we begin a session, your safe word is the only "wish" you will be granted! Use it wisely. This brings me to another aspect. Let us understand one another up front during our sessions - it is about your satisfaction, it is about your safety, it is about your compliance and submission, and it is about control. It is not about your humiliation, it is not about your self-esteem; I will not have you leave a session feeling humiliated - exhausted maybe but never humiliated.

In many ways I am pleased that I am not in the country, I would be too tempted to test you right now; too tempted to test your character and to test your resolve. You say that you love living on the edge; it appears that several of the things I mentioned excite you and amplify your thirst for more. This is good, extremely good. Let us see where this takes us.

You can give me the same exhilaration. What makes my heart pound? I would enjoy looking into your eyes and watching intently as you wonder what is next. This makes my heart pound, watching as your heart pounds excited and yes concerned. Knowing that in your head you have reached a paradox fearful with excited anticipation. This makes my heart pound. Sexually what do I enjoy, I love taking a woman anally, perhaps bound spread eagle on her stomach entering her in this position completely secured and firm, perhaps in a hood, perhaps masked with her eyes covered and warm oil over her entire body, glistening under candles as my genitals penetrate that place so taboo. Perhaps you would struggle just a bit and provide me an opportunity to spank your rear; yes this makes my heart pound. To watch your behind as it turns cherry and has the warm sting of a fresh spanking, that is most exciting. Even to run my tongue between your legs, spreading your labia so gently with my tongue inside you, probing you and preparing you for my entry.

All these things excite me Miselena, I am after all very visual, and I like to see a woman in a position that invites control. Silk teddies, thongs, g-strings - all very, very feminine. I am especially fond of sheer silk. To me it allows you to see but not see; it is explosive! To see the outline of your nipples or the shadow of your nipples but not completely exposed, wow! I also love the boy shorts. In my mind I can see you in a pullover gown, sheer and silky...

***

I have asked you to prepare yourself as I prefer. Always shaved, always a hint of fresh soap on your body! I come in and admire you in your sheer white gown and place your collar where it belongs. Your breasts are full and your nipples are already hard; you are excited and eager to begin. I grab your head (by your hair) into my hands firmly pulling your lips to me, a passionate kiss wet with excitement. Firmly I force you to your knees, (I imagine) you are so good at fellatio and I remind you what I want with one simple phrase, "Please me".

You take me into your mouth. I am shaved as you are, smooth and my skin is very tight. I am already quite thick and hard; you take me in slowly, teasing the crown of my penis with your lips and tongue, gently running your tongue the length of my shaft. "Enough"! I say and grab you by your shoulders to lift you to your feet, "Would you have this over so soon?" I grab your wrists and cuff you behind your back. I spread your legs wide open with my feet; you are still standing before me. Your gown is long and spreading your legs so far apart has the seams stretched as if they will split. I remove a pocket knife from my pocket; your eyes immediately widen and in your surprise you say "What"?

I do not even allow you to finish the sentence. I grab you by the arm and take you to the kitchen where I place you on your hands and knees; I temporarily unlock your cuffs and reattach them through the piping under the sink. You still have on your gown so I lift it to expose your behind. I have the cat with me; this time it stings. You count because you know it is your role and apologize for speaking with each stroke. You realize that this usually softens the strokes but gets you just as wet nonetheless. Finally done, I disconnect you and lift you up. We face each other; soft, deep and firm I say "Do you have anything else you wish to say"? Your only response is a soft shake of the head. Again I take out my pocket knife; I bring it between us and confirm to you, "You must trust me!" I spread your legs once again so wide you are off balance. Perfect! I lower the knife taking it down your body so that you feel the edge through your gown. Your breath is shallow and your nipples are incredibly hard. I stop long enough to circle each nipple allowing you time to feel the edge of the blade then continue past your navel to the tip of your clit. There I linger and once again take you into my mouth for a passionate kiss. The blade lowers and I thrust if forward cutting strips from your gown. "We will need these later."

Did you enjoy my little story Miselena?

As for fluids, I do enjoy a wonderful rub with oils all over my body... I would love someday to grind our bodies together dripping in oil with our sex sliding over each other.

As for your nighties I think I would take pictures of you in your night clothes. Especially your boy shorts.

Oh, and as far as semen I love to see hot semen being massaged into the breasts, especially over the nipples. It is a very erotic sight.

I do have a question for you though; I wish to hear you expound on your thoughts regarding self-esteem, control. I also want to know the extent of letting go only so far? Remember Miselena this is for our pleasure!

November 9

Oh D... you are good... where did you come from... and why ever did you pick me? You have set out on a path of discovering and uncovering those thoughts and desires I

34

have long kept to myself. Every letter probes a bit more; encourages me to reveal more, to give you more – and you do it in a manner that is totally intoxicating. The stories you weave and pictures you paint are erotic in the extreme; you take the thoughts I have expressed and incorporate them within the threads, increasing their intensity and their immoderate appetite for response... and respond I do for I cannot seem to resist seeking that which you so eloquently offer.

You speak of my making assumptions; I would beg to differ. No assumption was made regarding the desired outcome of climax; it was made regarding the expectation of that certain heart pounding exhilaration I have come to expect with your requests. I should have realized (and now do) that you have a purpose behind all your requests. I will not soon forget this seemingly single-minded devotion to my education to which you so consistently contribute. I also have no doubt the experience would be vastly different shared with you and indeed, attempted to allude as much.

You think perhaps that I will test your conviction... I had to smile... you are probably right. It isn't so much that I love to live on the edge but that I feel the need to push the edges of my reality to find out what the limits are. It is more of a controlled, conscious effort than a way of life for I only do so infrequently and generally with considerable forethought as to the potential outcome. Only if I can live with the outcome am I willing to proceed, so am I prepared? I will make certain that I am before I cross that line.

I find myself wondering how I will respond to you when we have our first real session. I am inclined to believe that shedding control will be an easy accomplishment for it is something you and I already know I seek... at least temporarily... and that you insist upon; so the ground rules are clear and firmly established. Will I pass your tests? I believe I will. I am submissive by nature; this much I have come to understand. I think I will be instinctively compelled to respond and will have to consciously choose to violate a rule. It is in my nature to want to please and if we succeed in going down this path for our pleasure, you will have that experience of me. That your understanding of this is so complete reassures me greatly that the faith I have already placed in you is well founded.

I am impressed, I have to say. You have listened (read) very carefully everything I have said and that you chose to do so as well as reiterate back to me those very things shows great compassion and interest in me personally. I thank you for that. And oh, my compliments to you... they are so well deserved...

You admonish me to remember that I will have no say in our sessions except to end them altogether. I will remember this but I will not be surprised if I surprise you. I think I will surprise even myself. Hmm... isn't that an interesting concept...

That brings up another comment you made... I disagree that this is about my satisfaction... I think it is about our satisfaction... for if you are not pleased with the result, it was not worthwhile in my estimation. I do agree that it is about my safety, for it is in you that I have to trust this to in this situation, and I will hold you to that. You have spent a considerable amount of time and effort to make me feel that anything between us would be in a safe and secure environment. I know you know I appreciate that (and need to hear it too). So that you do (understand and expend the effort) to do so, means a great deal to me and has made leaps and bounds in my trust level for you already.

You say that you are glad that you are not in the country for you would be tempted to test my resolve... phooey on that. I am eager for you to test my resolve... Indeed, until you do so, how am I ever to know what is to become of this great curiosity of mine? I have no one else with whom I express these feelings... you and you alone have had such uninhibited access to my deepest secrets, and mostly because I am struggling to be as honest with myself as with you. The positively worst lie you can tell is the one you tell to yourself and having decided to go down this path, I choose to do so with total and brutal honesty. The people who profess to know me would be shocked to read the things I have expressed to you. I am shocked at some of my more recent revelations, but I am determined to find out more; more about what this means and more about myself. You are a huge part of this for only you have made me think, question and examine those thoughts. And trust me when I say, I do all of those things.

You have answered my question so beautifully... that I can give you the same exhilaration you give me. It is so important to me that this (or any, for that matter) relationship is mutually beneficial or it simply will not go anywhere, and I have great desires for this to go as far as it is able for both our pleasure.

Did I enjoy your story? I *always* enjoy your stories. That is not to say that the introduction of a knife is going to bring me the same response as a previous acquaintance of yours, but I do believe that if and when we ever do have sessions, I will have found the ability to trust you implicitly. Indeed, I may already.

You ask about self esteem. This is a very complex subject and I have spent many, many years and lots of money attempting to better understand both myself and the reasons I do what it is that I do or have done in my life. Suffice it to say that my growing years and experiences contributed greatly to my sense (or lack) of self esteem and for many subsequent years I was bent on a path of self destruction. It is not a pretty picture and I really don't want to go there if it pleases you to allow me this indulgence. I am not bitter nor resentful for this life has made me who I am today and I am well pleased with where I have come, but I have no wish to revisit some of those times as they can be very painful. Perhaps we can speak of this sometime in the future if you really wish to know.

The extent of my only letting go so far has to do with control. Control over me, my actions, the repercussions for those actions and the lessons I have had to learn the hard way. Unfortunately, most of my lessons have come hard but life goes on and I am ever optimistic. Oh, and I rarely have to learn the same lesson twice...
Shall I send you a picture of me in my nightclothes?
~M

November 10

Miselena,

You always know just what to say. I picked you because I sensed you had a desire to dig deeper into your sexuality. Openness if you will, to see and explore the fantasies you've experienced. One thing that stuck out as I remember though is you wanted this without the sense of losing respect for yourself and that impressed me (it wasn't said in the ad that was just my assumption). I sense that you may have experimented in the past and either the results were not what you expected or the person wasn't the person you expected. In either event I appreciated the fact that we have picked each other and yearn for the opportunity to create that which we both desire. As I have said I have experienced before and it is an enlightening experience...

You mentioned that my request sometimes have underlying meanings - of that you can be assured. The sensations you feel are unique to you but when shared they will be different I assure you. The level of your previous experiences whatever they were will only serve as an introduction for us.

My dear of course you will test me, but I am encouraged by your natural ability to submit; I can hardly wait to take you to new limits and to experience with you the first time we experiment in areas previously untouched. You are right this is for both of us, for our pleasure. You will know immediately that which pleases me because my feedback will be instantaneous. By the same token I will correct whatever displeasure I have on the spot and I repeat, I do love a nice cherry behind. But the thing that excites me most is to watch as a woman submits all, the look, the expression when it is realized that a great deal of satisfaction will come from the pleasure we both have and in fact magnified by the pleasure we can give. You will give me great pleasure and I will ensure that I fulfill your desires because after all as you said if that is not the case we are doing it for nothing, and I do not want to waste your time or mine! It will be awesome because I will cherish your submission and hold it dear you may count on that!

This leads me to another thing you mentioned. It is with great pleasure that I assume the role of keeper of dark secrets, one of the few people that might know your dark side; the side that so few have seen, that in itself excites me. In fact that is one thing that will motivate us to new heights, the secrets we will share. Is it the taboo that excites you? Is it fear that excites you? Is it only your desire to please that will make you wet and allow me to take my pleasure?

As for those secrets that scar we will leave those where they are best kept! We will share our desires, we will quench each other's thirst for more and at the end of the day, we will revel in what we've accomplished and experienced. These things will be kept in the darkest part of our mind and when we are at work, or driving down the road we will grin to ourselves thinking "my goodness, I can not believe I did that" or even better "I can not believe that felt so good". No hang-ups, no judgment only honest pleasure this is what must be! This is for our pleasure!

As your lessons go, let's just say you might take pleasure in learning my lessons more than once. I think that you have in you something special, I want you to share. In fact during our sessions we will share many things over and over.

***

I can see you now dressed only in a gown, your head lowered, eyes to the floor and ready! I request that you remove your robe and replace your clothes with the items I have provided; a leather corset, heels, your collar. You put them on and you are stunning; sensual, erotic and ready. I grab you by the waist and turn you away from me. "Tonight we will explore anal play." Those words set off a warmth between your legs that surprises you. Unexpected yet anticipated. You've known that I do love a nice tight behind; tonight we will play with you there until you are ready to collapse with exhaustion. I have purchased many toys to prepare you this evening. I have several pillows that I lay on the floor, my concern for your comfort amazes you because you are aware how firm and strict I can be.

I would like you on your hands and knees and without question you kneel exposing your well rounded behind to me for exploration, slap, slap, slap, slap hard, stinging sharp slaps across your behind - it is enough to make me climax watching and feeling your warm behind under my hand, and I notice you are very, very wet! Noticing your moisture I stop the spanking and I take your clitoris between my thumb and forefinger squeezing and applying pressure to your swollen clitoris, squeezing harder and harder rolling your swollen clitoris under my fingers until I can feel your first shudder; the sight of you on your knees wet with your behind completely exposed is enough to cause me to explode.

Yes I like this sight, but instead I want to explore you back there where it is so taboo. I want to open you up for what is to come. I have hot oil; I squeeze it and it oozes between your cheeks and into your anus, your body is now glowing. I take a small butt plug and work it into your anal cavity, It slides in with more ease than either of us expect. I reach around to your nipples squeezing and rolling them until they are tender under my touch. I lift your eyes and show you my next toy. It is huge and you begin to shake your head pleading that I not try it. I smile and.......

Perhaps I will finish this one later...

Tell me Miselena have you ever worn heels?

Have you ever fantasized at work?

As for your nighties yes, yes, yes I would enjoy pictures of you in your night time clothes!

Oh and one more thing for me I do love to massage my semen into the skin, and I would love for you to accept my semen over your breast, hot and milky like a warm lotion and massage it into your breast, nipples and clit as you bring yourself to a warm climax.

November 11

Hello D,

It has been a long two days and I am glad to be finally answering your letter. I missed hearing from you today and know you are waiting to hear back from me; I have come to look forward to your correspondences with such anticipation that I apologize for the delay.

How lovely of you to express that I always know what to say... thank you. I have to smile though, for I spend a great deal of time on your letters, both in analyzing how I really feel about what you write and in composing an appropriate response so I am truly gratified that my letters are pleasing to you for I so enjoy yours.

Once again you have amazed me with your empathy. (I am starting to wonder how long you can sustain this D, lol...) I do have the desire to explore my sexuality and openness to entertain that which others might not. You have always been very forthright from the very beginning; very clear, open and honest yourself. You are consistent in your standards and values and it is for that reason I feel a certain comfort level in continuing down this path with *you*. You are to be commended D, for if I had any question you were anything other that what you have professed to be, I would have been long gone. The things we speak of require far too much faith to be entrusted to someone who is not worthy of that faith. Are you pleased... can you feel how much faith I have come to have in you already? And YES respect is important, respect, self-respect... all of it. You are incredibly respectful of me and I so appreciate that about you. Enlightening... Hmmm...

Now that leaves a lot of room for speculation...

You ask what it is about this that excites me... there are so many things... *you* for one... that the rules are so defined and the repercussion so instantaneous; it almost dares insubordination, that thrill of pushing your limits and getting away with it - that the rewards are also instantaneous; immediate gratification. That it is all about sensation and the collective focus is on pleasure with complete and total absence of outside influence;

an escape from daily pressure. That it has no expectations of and makes no demands on the rest of my life (actually that is more along the lines of appealing rather than exciting). That it is taboo? Not necessarily, what others call taboo I find interesting and appealing in its extremity. That it *is* extreme, that it is titillating, that it is intense. There are no judgments and no condemnation. That it is something I have never done before except in my mind and if the physical reactions to my imaginings are any indication, the reality could be explosive. Fear? Decidedly not; I don't do fear well (real fear), it is an emotion I am most uncomfortable with and won't even watch scary movies without coercion.

I love your vocabulary by the way; you have a lovely way of turning a phrase. Thank you for holding sacred that which I would share with you. And yes, you are certainly the keeper of my secrets.

Have I ever worn heels? Yes, almost every day in fact. Fantasized at work? Almost never... I am far too busy I'm afraid and find it difficult to shift gears so quickly should someone walk into my office.

There are so many pleasurable things I look forward to sharing with you D, and having you massage your semen into my skin will undoubtedly be one of them. I look forward to sharing your breath, your kisses, your caresses, your whispers... just the thought of these is enough to set my skin to tingling. I cannot begin to imagine what it will be like to sit across from you the first time. I want to be able to look into your eyes; I want to know what you see when you look into mine. I want to know if you are pleased with what you see and if you want to continue. I want to experience your sensuality and seduction, and I want it for our pleasure.

Attached are your pictures... or at least the ones of me tonight...
~M

November 12

Miselena,

Is everything going well with you?

November 12

 Ah ha! You must be awake where ever you are... and will have undoubtedly just gotten my email. D, do you ever use Instant Messaging? I will be online for a little while yet if you would like to chat...

~M
Oh, btw, it will show I'm not online but I will be... for a little while anyway.

November 12

Miselena,

What a thrill, watching you type real time on the other end. That was very nice! It is a shame that somehow we were disconnected. The possibility exist that this side was the problem, Europe is beautiful, and seductive but the states have the technology boom on lock... many things technology based are somewhat of a challenge for most of the countries over here, yes even today... I hope our brief communication did not disappoint you too much.

My goodness your behind is quite tempting and I would love to run my tongue the length of your sex, from the tip of your clit through your labia, pausing briefly to penetrate inside you tasting your sweet juice then completing my brief journey with a tease of each of your cheeks using the feathery tip of my wet tongue. I would of course return to the treasure between your legs, tasting, licking and penetrating you orally over and over and over. I would bring you to climax after climax only encouraged by the intensity of the previous spasm. Your body under my tongue would dance to the rhythm of my pleasure. Although there cannot be such pleasure without something to compare it to, so between moans of pleasure I would nibble and gently bite the meaty portions of your sex and following each nibble with the soft gentle caress of my tongue; the contrast will drive you wild. I would perhaps surprise you with a slip of my finger into your tight rectum, probing with lubrication in preparation for a bit of anal pleasure. I would take pleasure in your facial expressions as I stretch the rim of your anus with first one, then two, then three fingers while I bring you oral pleasure from the front.

***

Have you ever thought Miselena, how dark are your desires? I would enjoy tying you up, perhaps naked to a chair, tied so securely that your body takes the form of the chair, the legs, the back etc. From this position, with your arms secured, I would pull your hair back hard, you can feel the pressure at your roots. I would be naked by this point and my penis firm and rigid from the site of you patiently waiting for what I would have us do next. I would run my penis along your cheeks, my sex throbbing, so hot gliding across your face. I glide along your lips, leaving my thick pre-cum lubrication glistening from your cheeks.

"Taste it!" Your tongue slides out like a snake peeking out from its secure home, not quite sure the outside exposure will bring. "Taste it" I say again "I would like for you to please me Miselena" you hesitate with your response thinking what is in this for you... "Do you not take pleasure from my pleasure?" Still no response. "You will" I smile, as if I expected as much! You are almost defiant because seated I do not have ready access to spank and whip your behind. That does not halt my immediate response; I have a long stick with one short leather palate on the end, almost like a tongue. You've never seen this toy. I take the leather tongue and run it over your face, first down one side then the other... Your body is tingling with excitement... what will I do with this... I continue to run this stick/whip along your body, over your ears, down your neck so slow along the sensuous curves of your body. I lean over placing my soft lips over yours sharing the residue of my liquid on your lips. Again I raise my Penis to your lips, this time striking your lips with the crown of my thick head, leaving more pre-cum for us to share... gently slapping your cheeks with the full length of my penis, one last time passionately kissing you deep enough to cause you to squirm with excitement.

I ask "Miselena do you willingly accept what is to come" You only nod. The first gentle strike just misses the tip of your nipple; the leather tongue on my whip/stick has a dramatic effect when the leather strikes your nipples. It stings but your nipples swell with excitement... I alternate the strikes to make sure that you are able to adequately absorb the sensations you are feeling, your nerves so tender and on edge. Your areolas flush a deep pink as the blood rushes to the tips of your nipples. They are now so warm and tender you would beg me to spank your behind! "Would you please me now Miselena"? and you nod eagerly. I whisper in your ear, "I am not so sure Miselena; I think for now this pleases me more'.

I continue to run the stick/whip along your body, tracing your curves, stopping where your swollen clitoris extends beyond the flesh of your labia...You look at me, and I am smiling... the first strike takes you completely by surprise; although it is softer than the strikes to your nipples the sensation is incredible none the less... over and over, striking your labia and clit repeatedly.

Unbelievably you are getting extremely wet from this. I pull your hair back to kiss you full on your lips while striking your wet sex and you explode with the tremors that are the onset of your first climax. "Now you will please me" and with that you take me into your mouth, licking and sucking me while watching my face knowing that the sensation you are giving me is bringing me nearer to my own satisfaction. Once I am close I take my penis from your lips and finish what you have started so beautifully, spraying thick hot semen on your cheeks and nipples. I work this hot liquid into your nipples squeezing them hard under my thumb and forefinger, finally working my fingers down between your legs where I would bring you to a second climax. Your body is overwhelmed by the sensory flood you have been subjected to.

Mentally you are exhausted without even uttering a sentence, but this exhaustion is that filled with content. No penetration today, only bondage, but I am so pleased knowing that this night we have both taken certain pleasures! I bend over into your ear and whisper, "Perhaps we need more semen".

***

Miselena I will enjoy seeing you in heels, heels and your collar. As I began to say while we were attempting our instant messenger conversation, your tan is quite inviting and I can only imagine the contrast that exists between the cheeks in your behind. I will take much time there having pleasure over and over again, whispering in your ears how wonderful it is to be inside you, what a good submissive partner you are and the test you will come to expect and enjoy.

Miselena in day to day life do you wear panties? I mean normally when you are at work or around town? When you fantasize about your role, how are you referred to in these fantasies, in other words is your name used when you have extreme fantasies? In some cases the things we discuss are larger than life, i.e. you being the center, perhaps an exhibit, for multiple people, or multiple play, extreme anal play, toys these are the extremes that please me; give me just one extreme that pleases you!

Did you get my picture; it did take me some time to locate. For your next picture I desire a picture in similar clothing, but I wish you to spread your cheeks open inviting me for inspection.

I will await your response...

November 12

Good Evening Miselena,

I trust you had an eventful day and that you were able to consume the picture I provided (yes consume is an odd choice of words, however knowing the analytical part of you that I do, the word might be appropriate). Was it anything like you imagined? I have thought much about a sentence in one of your most recent emails and it has interested me, I would like for you to describe to me a scenario that you deem extreme in an erotic, sensual setting. After all what one might feel is extreme another might feel mundane.

November 13

Good morning D (or evening where you are),

I hope this finds you having an awesome day. I am traveling today (this afternoon) so I will be out of touch tonight and wanted to get something to you in the meantime. I'll be driving this week and it will be interesting to see how I feel as I come across scorched terrain.

I did receive your pictures, thank you, and as I had no preconceived notions on your appearance, I cannot say as to my imaginings.

I did enjoy IM for as long as we had it and the part of the message you missed was that you had entered my haven... very few people make it there for I guard it jealously. It was nice to share with you if only briefly.

If it pleases you, I am going to answer the questions in your letters today and will take some pictures and create scenarios for you over the weekend. (I am at work and do need to get back to it here pretty soon) Do I wear panties; almost never, even in day-to-day life and usually only for effect if I know I am likely to be intimate with someone. How am I referred to in my fantasies... good question. I don't know that I am referred to at all in a personal sense. I don't recall ever hearing my name mentioned but then it is something I have never thought of before. I will pay closer attention to this in the future and see if this becomes a bit clearer in my mind. One extreme that pleases me; first let me give you my definition of extreme, for there are many.

Main Entry: [1]**ex·treme**
Function: *adjective*
Etymology: Middle English, from Middle French, from Latin *extremus,* superlative of *exter, exterus* being on the outside
Date: 15th century
1 c : exceeding the ordinary, usual, or expected
So... based on this definition... you can probably see that there are many aspects of this that I might consider extreme... being blindfolded and being restrained are two that please me.

I will have more time this weekend to comply with your requests so look for an email from me soon.

November 16

Hi Miselena,

I am pleased that you were able to leave me a tidbit to nibble on while you are away for the weekend. I imagine the drive provided you with a paradox, drive and take the time to give thought to whatever events you experienced throughout your week and see the devastation that nature is capable of, or fly and get caught up in the normal business hustle, which includes being herded to whatever your next destination is. It is no wonder you choose to drive.

Now here is the part of the emails I always enjoy. responding to your inquiries and leaving you some of my own to ponder. Its kind of like Maslo's hierarchy of needs, once you've figured out that there is way more to physical sexual satisfaction than just thrusting movements, you realize that at some point there has to be a form of mental stimulation. You have stimulated me mentally and we will put the physical into action soon enough.

I will enjoy the pictures you send me in whatever position you are in and to be honest I hope that you enjoy taking them as much as I will enjoy seeing them! I trust you've noticed the change in the subject line that I have provided. I will take a moment to address a portion of that subject. Exhibitionism dear Miselena. Sometimes I get a sense that inside you there is a hidden part that would get extremely excited at the thought of being displayed perhaps naked in front of people, a crowd unable to identify you, to see your firm body, naked with your areolas and labia swollen with desire. Perhaps even spread eagle and bound to the bed while many stare at your immobile body admiring your sex, your helplessness, and showing their pleasure at how sensual and sexual you are. Yes exhibitionism my dear. Your face/Identity concealed, non-descript, not referred to in a personal sense at all!

***

You are present for pleasure and for pleasure only. Perhaps I would release one hand and encourage your self-satisfaction. Yes masturbation, you pleasing yourself as I whisper to you how pleased I am. I will fill your head with the thoughts of the people that watch you as you bring yourself to climax after climax. Finally I would restrain your wrists once again and bring to the forefront of the crowd a female. I would tell you that this person has never tasted a woman (of course I have someone in mind). She has requested to taste your sex, but you must not move while she experiments on your body. You lie there like a mannequin, so still, so receptive. She probes you timid, and apprehensive. You can tell she has never done this; her tongue feels clumsy inside you yet so soft and gentle. You see her raise her head and look to me saying "your submissive's juices taste so sweet, I could do this all night", this creates your first oral explosion.

I speak to you telling you how proud I am and how pleased this makes me. The woman continues, running her tongue around the rim of your anus then darting inside you; she is exploring every inch of your sex. Her hand drifts between her legs to massage her own desires while she continues to perform oral on you and with your sex in her mouth she screams from her own orgasm. She is done and lifts up to kiss you, but I remind her that this is not permitted, "the lips are only for our pleasure". A man steps forward from the crowd; he is naked from the waist down, his penis is dark and huge. It is obvious what his desires are but I remind him of the rules and he understands; he masturbates inches from your face, looking at your body and wanting intimacy but unable to touch (as he would like).

I suggest that he take his pleasure out on the woman that has just performed oral on you. She bends over in front of you taking your nipple into her mouth while he enters her from behind. You can feel the power of his thrust even though she is only sucking your nipples; he announces that he is ready - he pulls out and sprays his warm semen over your body. Another gentleman copies this performance, then another and another until your body is covered with hot semen; you have done remarkably well, lying there still unmoving, I am so proud of you.

It is now my turn but the lips are mine; you take me eagerly into your mouth and it feels like heaven. This sight again draws the woman to you and while you are performing fellatio on me she displays two nice sized dildos; the guys are drooling because they wanted so badly for it to be them. She continues using the toys to fill each of your orifices. You feel my head swelling in your mouth which triggers your own release, we explode together.

***

Miselena have you ever had sex outside in the public? Somewhere secluded but open at the same time? Have you ever been in your car naked from the waist down? I will admit this one is fantasy. To have a woman on the open road remove her blouse, completely naked from the waist up, and as we drive by the late night truckers she sits as if nothing is abnormal but we notice the truckers trying to keep pace as we get bored with one. What a thought?

How was your weekend?

I will have some interesting questions for you tomorrow!

D

November 16

Hello D,

I *was* an interesting drive and very sobering to see the extent of fire damage; you can actually still smell it in the air and I wonder how long that will last. Next week I fly and then drive for Thanksgiving weekend but you are correct in that I find an appreciation for the journey, both in time to think and to relax. Oh... and yes by the way, I have driven without a blouse/top on and have found the other drivers on the road to be totally oblivious...

Thank you once again for the compliments. I am pleased that you find my letters thought provoking for I do yours as well; indeed I do believe that provoking is the perfect word for this last one. I am curious, I must admit. What is it in my letters that sometimes gives you the sense that I might find exhibitionism exciting? That I would choose to display myself for and allow liberties with total strangers? It is exceedingly apparent to me that this is an activity you find appealing simply by the number of times you have chosen to bring it into our conversations but I'm not sure at all where you might be interpreting my interest. This last scenario involves a great many people and while after many, many letters I might be inclined to trust you, I am not at all certain I would trust or feel safe in the situation you have described. The one appealing thing I did find was that there was something reserved for our pleasure only. Perhaps simply not multitudes of people D, one might be appealing... I don't know. I have to think about this some more (and I will).

Have I ever had sex outside in public... no. Have I ever been in my car naked from the waist down? No, but as I mentioned, certainly from the waist up. I think I must be a study in contradiction... there are parts of me that are extremely conservative and others that are screaming to get out. It is difficult for even me to know what I am truly uncomfortable with unless the subject arises and I have an opportunity to think on it.

The pictures I have included are based upon your original request for similar clothing and a particular position; I hope you find them pleasing. I have to mention however, that you may not find tan lines, lol, as I generally tan without the benefit of a suit. There may be some that are slight, but I am fairly tan over all of my body.

And now I do believe that I owe you a scenario... let's see... the parameters were I believe something extreme in an erotic, sensuous setting...

***

It is night and warm as only the desert can be so late in the evening. You have dressed me tonight, as is your want, in heels, my collar, a thong and a diaphanous top, long sleeved with a scooping neckline but short... only extending to my ribs just below my breasts. It is blue I think, but so dark a blue as to be almost black. "Beautiful" you whisper and lead me by the hand outside.

The stars are out in all their glory and dimmed not at all by the candles placed so carefully in and around the patio. You have taken such care to create an atmosphere of magic... soft, instrumental, exotic music, perfumed candles whose fragrance, sweet and fleeting floats on the slightest breeze. 'Tropical', I think to myself, even though we are miles from the nearest ocean.

You lead me to a chaise lounge and stand me before it; you are standing so close behind me I can feel your breath on my neck. "Don't move from where I place you" is whispered in my ear as you gently run your fingers down my arms and lift them from the hands straight out to my side. "Close your eyes" you say softly, and I resist for I can't bear to leave the beauty of the scene you have so carefully created but slowly, too slowly they close. Already the familiar warmth is spreading throughout my body and the tingling has begun.

"You hesitate" you whisper... "I wonder why". I know better than to speak, but that you have noticed my hesitation sends shivers down my skin for I know well the consequence of that hesitation and my heartbeat picks up speed. "Do you wish to please me Miselena?" you breathe against my neck. I nod yes... "Then don't hesitate again for I have only so much patience". Again I nod.

Slowly I feel your hands running over my body. Your fingertips are so light as to tease the skin and they explore every inch as if you had never touched me before or would never again. You move close behind me, leaning your body into mine and your arms reach around and cup my breasts grasping my nipples with your fingers. Gentle at first, the pressure increases steadily until I am gasping and you whisper "did you think of me like this when I had you perform your exercises?"

"Yes", I answer, forgetting I am not to speak.

"Bend over and place your hands on the lounge."

Immediately I tense and then bend over as required and force myself to relax. Instinctively I know that to be tense will increase your displeasure. "Ten" you whisper as you caress my rear... and I wait...

"One" I start to count as your hand lands so firmly on my behind, "two", and so on until I have completed the count and now my rear is hot and red.

"Stay", you say, "I have not given you permission to move" and I comply without question. Slowly you peel off my thong; it feels rough over my sensitive skin and you lift my feet free of it. Moving your hands up my legs, you open me from behind and glide your tongue ever so gently along my labia to my anus taking your time and easing the soreness you have caused. It is almost too much, this pleasure you now bestow upon me and sensing this, you stop. "Not yet" you whisper...

Now D... what would you do next?

~Miselena

November 17

Welcome back sweet Miselena,

I am just curious about a couple of things (well ok more than a couple but I'll only address a couple today...) do you read these emails mostly at night or during your day? Second do you find yourself at your sexual peak at night or during the day, or doesn't it matter? Just curious.

Well in your email you mentioned you have tried the driving with your breasts exposed, very erotic and most adventurous (exhibitionism) Did the driving sans top excite you, or did you just do it to see the reaction you would receive? What were the circumstances surrounding this adventure? I think it would please me to experiment with this at some point. I think I would find it pleasing to see the reaction others might have if they stopped to see your rosy areolas exposed. I would prefer to have you masked in our scenario or perhaps even in a wig to disguise your identity.

As for your belief that I am occupied with the thoughts of multitudes of people - it is not the thought of people that occupy me - it is the thought of your reaction that I desire. You see, I will take pleasure at some point (if we proceed) in watching you either being pleased or pleasing someone for me. This pleasure may be as simple as directing you to strip naked (masked of course) while you are admired for your beauty and grace. There will be no sex involved, however I do wish to watch your reaction as I give direction and you obediently follow. This will only happen after and if you feel comfortable with our exploration. If you recall, I said before and will always say, This is for our pleasure. If it is not pleasing to both of us, it will not happen! It is as simple as that.

Now does that mean I will not stretch your imagination and your reality; I will do that and so much more! I will take you to the edge and Miselena you will beg for more, when you are ready, but not before! I hope we are clear on that because it is extremely important to me that you understand you will be taken to higher levels of pleasure, but it must be gradual and at the time of our choosing. So when you say I seem to take pleasure in the multiples, it is your pleasure that will give me pleasure. It is your ecstasy I seek! However, I only want these things if they can be achieved by US exploring a path not normally traveled. Now let me explain; I'm not talking about anything ridiculous like standing naked under the moon, and howling or anything that is truly painful, or dangerous, but I do want to ride the line of extremities you mentioned in your email... Although now that I think of it, some would call anal sex extreme. I believe that is only an introduction.

Miselena you are indeed a work in contradiction and I like it because somewhere within the contradiction lies your true desires. You have many attributes that one would consider conservative, to include your language. You are extremely articulate, seldom reverting to using proverbial phrases like "fuck", "ass", "dick" or "pussy". I enjoy reading your every email and appreciate your command of the English language; I will take even greater pleasure of your conservative nature when I am inside your mouth, vagina or anus. Why? Because your intelligence pleases and excites me! But there is another side of you we seek! This is the side that will do as I command without hesitation or apprehension (I know, I know, yes we will get there). This is the side that will play with the illusion of bondage! This is the side that will kneel and please me orally over and over. This is the side I will discipline. This is the side that will eagerly receive my nipple pain and pressure. This is the side that will be waxed and prepared. This is the side to which I will whisper sweet gentle commands to be instantly obeyed. The only question will be is this the side you want to share "for our pleasure"?

Miselena have you ever been spanked with a paddle?

The finish to your story:

***

I whisper in your ear, "I thirst, do not move". We have a bottle of wine, a Merlot comes to mind. I pull your head back firmly by your hair, grasping a handful as if I were attempting to pull it out by the roots. This creates a natural arc in your spine that is a perfect wine receptacle. As I pour the wine the chill causes you to naturally jump, you look back to see if this reaction will draw retribution from me; only the firm pinch of your nipples to help you maintain your focus! I continue and you remain still without movement. The wine flows from your shoulder blades down your spine; you believe I have poured too much as the amount is excessive and continues down between your cheeks, but this is where I want it! I remain behind you and lick the wine from the tip of your clit up around your anus, up to the receptacle formed by the arc in your back, over your spine to your neck and shoulders. My tongue like a light feather glancing over your skin.

I ask if you are thirsty, you nod a response. Suddenly warm water is poured over your head; like a gentle caress the water flows over your cheeks, not too hot, not cold at all; "you may drink". Your sex is now dripping wet, and I ask if I may taste the sweet mixture of the juices that flow from you and the wine I have poured. You know the only correct response is a nod; I proceed to take your labia into my mouth, sucking, pulling them gently inside my own. My nose is buried between your cheeks while I drink your juice as if to quench my dying thirst. "Miselena you taste so good." Again you are on the brink and I feel the shudder as if your own climax has begun.

Slap a hard, firm slap on your behind arouses you; this one stings because the wine has your skin wet. I whisper in your ear "do not test me again sweet Miselena, you will receive your reward soon enough". I take hold of your arms, keeping them firm to your side and lift you up from your position to face me directly. I lift you onto the table and spread your legs as wide as they could possibly be; in your mind you think "finally penetration". Hard, stiff penetration. I lean over to passionately kiss you and it brings a warmth over your body that only serves to increase the excitement occurring between your legs.

You feel me probing as if to enter but not your vagina! I took the opportunity while behind you to lubricate my throbbing penis. It only takes a second and the head is lodged tightly in your anus, you gasp because the head is so thick. The only words you hear from me at this point surprise you. "Miselena your ass is always so inviting" My thick penis is so tight inside you that it feels as if we will both explode. I have a small leather strip in my hand and I begin gently slapping it against your swollen clit, gentle yet firm then harder and harder and harder. At first it is quite uncomfortable but at the same time unusually exciting. I am deep inside you by now and as I look down I see that your excitement has your vagina wide open, it is as if I can see the very insides of your body. I continue to slap your swollen clit while thrusting deep inside your bowels. Your nipples swell with excitement and the sight of my muscular body over you... with one hand I have your nipples between your fingers applying pressure, harder and harder with every anal thrust. Your labia are now pink from a combination of excitement and whipping. I say "Oh she looks like she deserves a sweet kiss" I bury my head into your sex and once again bring you just to the brink of climax. The next thing you hear is "Miselena I would like for you to please me before I allow you to finish" Do you think you can please me? "If you please me you will be allowed to cum." You look at my swollen penis, clean shaven, smooth, completely hairless. I ask again, "Do you think you can bring this to my pleasure?"

***

Tonight Miselena I would like you to spread your labia apart and gently tap them with the inside portion of your hand glancing over your clitoris, steadily increasing speed and intensity until your clitoris is swollen and tender. I want you to think "during our sessions I will share all that I have!"

Thank you Miselena for the pictures they are perfect. I will have you in this position over and over, completing our sessions with sensual sex that is meant for us only. No matter what else is done, when we are finish playing the sensual touching will be yours and mine alone!

Do you enjoy Jazz Miselena?

What scents do you enjoy (Cologne/Perfume)?

Miselena, close your eyes and picture yourself bound with a candle on your stomach in a holder... You are blindfolded but you know it is there. The room is silent save soft music in the background. You can not tell if I am still there or not; you want to peek, the curiosity is killing you. You believe you can position yourself to take a quick survey of the room; however you know If you move the wax will drip and sting your flesh. As long as you stay still you are fine....what would you do?

I want to know more of what contradictions you have!

Welcome back and write soon

November 19

Hello D,

I hope this finds you well and loving life in Europe. Thanksgiving is next week and I wonder what you will do to celebrate; as I recall, no one over there recognizes that particularly American Holiday. Will you miss being home?

You have a great many questions in this email so I will set out to answer each one of them in turn. When do I read your emails? Whenever I notice they have arrived... that can be either at work or at home, but it doesn't stop there for I re-read them often as well.

I'm having a lovely glass of Pinot Noir; wish I could share a glass with you...

Sexual peak... hmmm... yet another topic I haven't given any thought to before this. I suppose it doesn't matter; what I do know is that I tend to have cycles where I am either more or less focused on my physical pleasure. When I am in 'heat' so to speak, I want to make love all the time and the time of day generally bears no consideration. By the same token, when I'm not, I can take it or leave it altogether and it makes little difference. What provokes this? I haven't a clue so it must be physiological.

Did driving without my blouse excite me? Yes, but then I was in one of my cycles and it doesn't take much (actually that's a lie; it doesn't take anything) to get me excited because my body just seems to have a mind of its own at that point. What were the circumstances? It was the middle of summer and the temperature was in the 100's; the air conditioning was out in my car and it is a long, hot drive in the desert without air. I was using ice water to keep me cool and I wanted to feel it against my skin and not through my top... so... I peeled it off... As I recall, that is the same trip I did the wax from the picture you have seen... yes, on the road.

Again you are truly generous with your compliments; thank you. I am glad my writing and intelligence are pleasing to you. I did get your IM messages as well and was very pleased to hear you enjoyed my story. I did enjoy writing it and found that it was a very welcome test of my creativity. It is not likely however, that we will connect on IM as long as you are in Europe though, for your messages come in at about 2:00 in the morning and I am almost never awake then.

Is this the side I want to share (the side that instantly obeys your commands)? Yes, this is precisely the side that I want to share and explore and I do believe you are quite capable of directing that pleasure. You are very direct, firm, determined and in control. It is extremely appealing, this mastery you exude and I often wonder what our first meeting will be like.

Have I ever been spanked with a paddle? No I have not; what is it you prefer?

Oh, and you liked my most recent pictures... that is good; I am glad you were pleased.

And I can now tell you that when I fantasize/masturbate, I am called by my own name, no pseudonyms.

Do I enjoy jazz; no, I am not particularly fond of jazz. For making love I like some of the more exotic instrumentals; Enigma is particularly good and although that is not instrumental, it is very sexy music. I like something with a good beat and exotic instruments.

For pleasure I listen to a very wide range of music, from classic rock to contemporary Christian... very bizarre... and some more of the contradiction so inherent to my nature.

Cologne (perfume)? I prefer Versace; I particularly like Woman and Versus, and while I know you like the smell of soap, I prefer the scent of perfume on my body (I'm quite sure that must be a girl thing).

Last question... what would I do? That is an easy one. I am very good at patience and controlling my curiosity. I often drive people crazy with the length of time I can drag out opening a present and even do so just to get that very reaction on occasion. There is something about savoring the anticipation.

Contradictions... I have many and wouldn't even know where to begin but as we go I am sure more and more of them will surface. Now D, what can I do next for our pleasure? What would you have of me?

~Miselena

November 20

Miselena,

How are you? This email is particularly appealing for many reasons however I will begin with Season's Greetings. Thanksgiving is a wonderful time of year it makes us take a moment and even if only during the dinner give thanks for what we've received throughout the previous year. I will undoubtedly miss being home during this time my itinerary for this period is a bit hazy, I have been requested to travel to Dubrovnik, however several things may preclude this travel. In any event I will be in one of several places, yes still over here. I have acquired an affinity for calamari di fritti (fried calamari) but just can't bring myself to have that for a Thanksgiving meal so I will probably dine in typical Thanksgiving fashion. What of your plans will you have a big spread for Thanksgiving?

I enjoyed this email as much as any. Oh and before I forget, you did not complete your previous tasking. (Does the number "10" ring a bell, or make you tingle.) I wish to know if you slapped your labia as I requested. If you were unable to comply a response is appropriate (requesting forgiveness of course). If you did comply with my request provide me the details of the scenario and the physical sensations you experienced.

Wine, wine, wine... Pinot Noir, that's nice. I am south of Tuscany a region rich in wines, particularly Chianti's. Perhaps when I return we will share not only a glass but perhaps an entire bottle. Oh this has reminded me of my story. Did you enjoy the story? We will play out the wine portion most definitely and I imagine since I love perform oral as a teaser I will complete at least that portion of the story, how I wish I could taste your sex even today.

"Timing is everything" you mentioned that timing has no bearing on your sexual drive or intensity. I thoroughly enjoy the use of the word heat. We will explore that more at another time.

Ah the blouse so tell me did the truckers pay any attention to the fact that a beautiful lady passed them by, sans blouse? In your day to day activities do you wear a bra? You will not wear one for our first meeting, nor will you wear panties (which I believe is your normal practice). You obviously did not do the wax on the highway but that is a tempting thought. Oh and since we are on the subject of your pictures, I enjoyed a nice round of masturbation while viewing the pictures you sent. Specifically the pictures that had you posed on your hands and knees. I could just make out your nipples swollen and pink in the front and your firm rear end; the sight was quite appealing and sexual.

Yes, I thoroughly enjoy your intelligence and the expanse of your vocabulary, but I will admit, by the very nature of our desires our sessions may draw out more a basic, animalistic side of your persona, and I hope you are prepared to deal with that. Miselena,

I am pleased that we share the same desires or that our different desires create a symbiotic relationship.

I enjoy being in control, directing with an expectation of complete obedience. I also hold a leadership position in my day to day life but I enjoy the feeling of being in complete control without question. This is only capable on a personal level where trust has been established. Yes I too think that I am perfect for what you seek because once our sessions begin I will not allow you the pleasure of decisions. A choice will be given to you at the beginning of each session; once committed the only other choice will be to stop that session. I know this excites you and to be quite honest it excites me as well. I will always begin by presenting you a choice, once you have accepted I will dictate the direction and course of that session.

Once we do meet (yes I know "when will this ever happen") I think there will be instant chemistry. Although I will keep true to my word, and our first meeting will most likely occur during the day over coffee, I will add a small twist (since you enjoy surprises I will leave that one for later) not to worry it won't be too intrusive or obvious to anyone but you and me.

I have yet to decide if I will call you Miselena during our sessions. I am inclined not to. I want to take you as far away from your daily persona as I can. I know it appears that you are an enigma, a contradiction. I will remove that confusion for you. During our sessions you will be who we wish you to be, and there will be no contradictions, no confusion. Where I take you will be clear and decisive if you allow it. If I do decide to call you by some other name during these sessions (and whatever is chosen will be the same for each session) rest assured that while it will be respectful in nature, there will be no doubt that I am in control.

What would I have you do for our pleasure? What are you capable of? No do not answer; that will come soon enough. We will have all that we both desire and you will do more than you ever thought possible. For now here is my request; I would have you purchase a ping pong paddle, an everyday item that can be found at any K-mart, Wal-Mart, Big-5, or Sports Authority. I want you to find an opportunity to test it for me. I want you to spank your behind with this paddle until it stings, thinking of the contradictions you have presented me with. I want you to think of the ways we will please each other, without contradiction for our pleasure. I want you to think of how you will release yourself to my care when we are together. I want you to spank your behind and when you feel it is at a point that would satisfy me, I want you to masturbate with the handle resting between your labia (sitting on the handle, straddling it if you are able) and fantasize about me whispering in your ear. If you have an opportunity a picture of your behind without panties bent over for me to review as if I am inspecting your wondrous body, this would be pleasurable to me.

By the way to answer your question I enjoy skin to skin contact, when I spank your behind I want to feel your flesh under my hand. I want to feel the heat of your skin. So I will enjoy spanking your behind with my hand. I believe this is because I am as sensitive as I am dominant (I guess my own contradiction). I enjoy the sensuality of the moment, I enjoy the erotic, exotic side of domination, and soon enough we will enjoy each other.

As I think about this I would love to see your body under the glow of candle lights, perhaps glistening after you have rubbed hot oil over your entire body. I would perhaps arrive, require you to disrobe and provide you oil to rub into your body, for our pleasure making sure that you cover every inch. I would instruct you to touch places that please us most, inserting my fingers into your vagina and rectum while your hands glide over your own skin teasing your body for our pleasure. I would be whispering into your ear, my hot breath caressing your skin like a warm feather, and when I feel you are prepared to explode I would firmly grasp your neck in my hand and remind you "only when I have permitted release, after all my dear would you please yourself without pleasing me?" You shake your head.

I remove my penis from my pants, running it along your cheeks, slapping your face with my rigid member, not hard but enough to remind you that it is there and will require your attention! I would ask, "Are you hot yet"? You nod. I retrieve the ice tray from the refrigerator. I place a cube between my lips and run it the length of your neck, down to your waiting vagina. I have placed the ice cube under my tongue and I now have your clitoris in my mouth. As I roll the ice cube from under my tongue and slide it inside your wet vagina you jump, it is so cold, but I continue to lick and suck your clitoris until you body begs for release. I look up at you and with one comment "You have been good this night, and I approve" you explode in my mouth!

Miselena do you own a pair of tight jeans?

Write soon with the result.

November 22

Hello D,

It is 11:00pm on Saturday and you will have said goodbye to this day long ago and started Sunday by the time you get this. It has been a long day for me and I think that is the kindest thing I can say tonight. I'm looking forward to getting back tomorrow.

I owe you a letter and answers to a few more questions, and I thought that this might be a good way to wind down from the day.

As to exercises and negligence... I did neglect to mention in my email any details about your request and my experimentation and yes, that was intentional. Not because I was attempting to avoid the subject but because I have not yet found the time to complete this task to its full potential. I have played with it, yes but my days (and evenings) have been so busy this past week that I simply haven't had the time to devote the right frame of mind and atmosphere to it. Until I do, I won't be able to comply with your request properly.

It was my feeling that this would be a disservice to our emails as this is for our pleasure and every effort I make should be my best, not half-baked. I am hoping to find the time and quiet and focus to do this tomorrow, (really hoping, lol). Needless to say, neither have I had the time to purchase a ping pong paddle and can't even begin to think when I might. I honestly don't think it will be anytime in the next week as my next ten days are lining up to be as busy as my last ten. So... all I can do is beg your indulgence.

Does the number '10' make me tingle? Oh yes and I believe you already know it does. Why is that; why is it that just the thought of that is enough to make my heart start beating, my limbs start to tingle and the blood run to my behind and labia making me warm and aching for attention. I am so often caught by one simple sentence or phrase in your emails that has such a profound effect on me physically. It blows me away sometimes and yes, I am most curious as to what this is all about and where it will lead and just how you will direct it.

Did I enjoy your story; yes, I love your stories and this one was beyond the pale in intensity. I get hot every time I read it and I don't believe you would have had to ask me twice, never mind three times. I would like it very much if you would explain a few of the more subtle rules to me. Your stories sometimes leave me wondering what finer points am I as yet, unaware.

Did the truckers notice me at all? Not that I could tell but then driving for hundreds of miles in the desert will make anyone semi-numb to the cars passing you. You just get into a kind of zone out there after a while. I guess that is part of why I like the drive; while you're keeping an eye on traffic, you're really watching the scenery go by and some of it is absolutely spectacular.

Do I wear a bra? Almost always and yes, your instructions came through loud and clear; I will abide by your wishes.

You enjoyed the pictures; I am so pleased. I am hoping to work on your next request tomorrow and have already started to formulate some ideas on how I want this to turn out. Something with all your thoughts, I think; candlelight, oil, we'll see.

Am I prepared to deal with a more basic, animalistic side of my persona? The honest answer is that part of me is and part of me hasn't the foggiest notion of how I'm going to really feel once I'm there. I guess what matters is whether I am willing to find out whatever it is that this experience will bring out in me. And I am definitely ready to take a few more steps in that direction.

Yes, I believe you just may be perfect and we will see just how far we will go together. That you will be in control is no question in my mind and that I will be obedient as well and yes, the thought excites me very much. I have so many delicious pictures floating in my head from all the letters you have written.

Do I own a pair of tight jeans? I suppose that depends on your definition of tight. I own lots of jeans and most of them are snug but I'm not sure I would use the word tight; I don't find them very comfortable if they are too tight and they are some of my very favorite comfort clothes.

I hope your Sunday is wonderful D; do you get a chance to take time off to explore? Do you explore? What do you like to do with your free time over there?

~Miselena

November 23

Wow Miselena are you always up this late? It sounds like your day was full of adventure, not the kind we would have but exhausting all the same. Remember Miselena whatever you owe me I will have. One sentence below draws my attention and instant pleasure "I beg your indulgence". There may come a time (sooner rather than later I hope) that you will beg for more than indulgence. You may beg for penetration, you may beg for release, you might even beg for mercy (after all you are up to 20). We will see!

I will admit I do at some level appreciate your desire to give your response the attention it deserves. I will agree, a half-baked response would not meet my approval and would leave us both dissatisfied. So you prepare as necessary and I will impatiently await your response. By the way, make sure that when you purchase the paddle it is sturdy in nature, we will use this together at some point.

There will be many things you do for our pleasure and they will cause you to re-examine your thoughts and your desires. Miselena make no mistake, for what time we share during our sessions you will be mine and I will have no problem controlling and directing the scene.

I will wait to see what you have for me. Ultimately I am certain you will fulfill all my desires and expectations, even those that you believe you have to give thought to. I trust I will do the same for you, for as you so eloquently put it "if it is not for our pleasure it is for nothing". I know there will be initial apprehension but your trepidation will fall away under my commands like a silk scarf.

I will disrobe your clothing first, then your consciousness, and all that I see will be mine for our pleasure! I will fondle, caress, kneed and even discipline your breast if that is what is necessary. I will suck, lick, massage and penetrate your sex to bring you to climax after climax, but my intent is to cause you to understand better the hidden desires that you have. Admit it or not, you are as curious about discipline and bondage as you are about submission! We will be tender and explore them all. We will be pleased by each other; your obedience and my direction. I will have you bow, kneel, masturbate, and display yourself completely to me.

You will remove my clothes, and provide me oral satisfaction, giving every inch of your body to our desires. I will watch as you take hold of another's penis in your hand bringing it to full attention (nothing less is acceptable) and watch the ensuing explosion without thought as I bring you to your own climax. I will watch as you spread your legs and receive oral satisfaction from another female while I whisper the beauty of the sight before me. Your contradiction is amusing for I will choose the mood, music, apparel and language during our pleasure; there is no room for contradiction. I will whisper direction so soft, and sensual in your ear; "Spread your pussy open for it pleases me". The only accepted response is a nod; the faintest hint of hesitation will solicit an immediate response from me. Our relationship during these times will be clear and you will come to crave them like a drug, but I will take care to measure your indulgence. We will know each other in many ways on this level, but this level alone. I will come to you like a thief, and steal your reality, bringing your fantasy to life.

You ask how the first meeting will be. You and I know it is only a formality. Yes I will have you perform for me this first day, but as I have said it will be transparent to all but you and me. The first encounter will be brief, I will leave your heart pounding with excitement and anticipation for the earliest opportunity when you will kneel and submit.

I know I have given you much to contemplate, and many decisions to ponder but we both know there is only one conclusion you can come to, acceptance! Acceptance that I will take care to ensure your safety, acceptance that I will keep this completely discreet, acceptance that we will both be pleasured by the experience and acceptance of my control.

There will be many times that I will spank and paddle your ass until it is warm and very, very tender to my touch, alternating that sensation with the silky hot warmth of my tongue and mouth. Your nerve endings will feel as if tiny fires have been ignited under your skin shooting wave after wave of pleasure and pain to your consciousness. Your non verbal communication will tell me to stop but your eyes will beg me to continue until we are both exhausted mentally and physically. We talk of extremes but how do we measure them. I will tell you, your extremes will be measured by the dildos, whips, paddles, weights, clamps and ropes; these will be the tools of our measurements.

What do I do? I enjoy motorcycles and running. Like you I enjoy hitting the road and taking in the natural beauty, smells and people around me. Like you I work constantly and so I do not take advantage of this as often as I would like but when I have a few moments I make every effort to get out and enjoy my surroundings.

Now you, what do you do when not working so hard? It appears your time is a premium and you say you do not enjoy sports (which I find hard to believe seeing that you are in awesome shape) so what do you do?

Next email: Boundaries and Sex

November 24

Hello D,

No, I am normally an early to bed kind of person and Saturday was the result of lots to do and being keyed up from all the activity. I am back now and safely ensconced in my abode away from all the noise of the world. And yes, it is without a doubt a haven for me. It is early afternoon and I have the rest of the day to fulfill your requests; there are three if I am not mistaken and if it pleases you, I will accomplish them in the order requested beginning with my labia. Spread them and tap with the inside of my hand, increasing speed and intensity. The first thing was to erase all other influences and allow myself to get into the right frame of mind and so, I hope you will be pleased to know that I went to your letters. They engage my mind on so many levels and they are all intoxicating.

It was clumsy at first until my hands felt comfortable and I could block out what I was doing and concentrate on how it felt and then it was merely interesting for the next minute. But then, as I picked up speed and increased the intensity, the sensations started to flood my body. My labia and my clitoris were getting warm, very warm and my clit was beginning to throb. My heartbeat kicked in and my breathing became a sensation of its own; deep gasps sending tingles down my skin in full body rushes. The more I increased the intensity, the sharper the contrast between the sting and the warmth and I found that I liked them both very much. I am even throbbing now just thinking on it and when I was done, positively aching for release. I think I would have exploded if you had touched your mouth to me at that moment. I think I will like it even more when I am restrained and cannot control the strength and the tempo. Then you will have me begging for our pleasure, as is your want. I would have begged if you were here today.

And the ping pong paddle; well D, I hope you are smiling because I got that done too. I actually went into a store and purchased it. I recall having to fight to keep from blushing... and no, lol... I didn't buy the one with sandpaper... but they come nicely padded these days with smooth rubber surfaces. Not at all like I remembered from my youth. The experience... felt a bit silly I'm afraid and oh, loud... so loud in fact, I began to wonder if my neighbors could hear because I can certainly hear them on occasion. And so sweet (kind, considerate and forgiving... lol) D, I chose the path of discretion. I don't want my neighbors wondering what goes on in my apartment. I don't even want them to know if I am home. I simply don't want to be disturbed here in any way... (I know, it sounds a little extreme but there it is...) Perhaps you will be pleased to know that I did continue for a short while and the warmth and tingling it produced was very pleasant... and yes, pink anyway if not cherry. I actually took your pictures after and I believe the lighting picked it up in one of the shots. If it pleases you to be indulgent in this, I would be greatly appreciative.

And then the request for new pictures; you will already have figured out that I accomplished this as well. I do hope you are pleased with my efforts.

What do I do with my leisure time? Well, I don't ride motorcycles as much as I used to so I envy you that, but I do like to ride off road when I have the opportunity and have done some respectable mountain ranges. I love to read; I spend a fair amount of time these days in reading your letters and responding to you, and what a pleasure that has been. I respond to you on so many levels, physically, mentally and in correspondence (more about today's letter to come...). I find I am enjoying writing, lol... you raise the bar for me there as well. I don't watch much television but I like movies. I've actually been known to watch four movies in a row; those are days when you know I had to be wiped out and needing to recoup. Oh, and I love the occasional trip to Mexico. I will have a house on the Sea of Cortez someday.

This last letter is perhaps the most powerful letter you have yet sent incorporating a subtly altered tone that is slightly edgier. A written spanking, if you will (that may be a little severe but I don't think it is too far off). You must have felt I needed one; or a fresh dose of reality when it comes to what you will and will not allow. I would like to make one point though, if I may; my contradictions are what I am attempting to face head-on, not hide behind. You have given me a lot to consider and have certainly been forthcoming in your expectations of me. Part of what you have written excites me greatly... part of it scares me and I have to remind myself to trust that you will set the pace gradually.

Your next subject, Boundaries and Sex? I can't wait.

~Miselena

November 25

Miselena,

My goodness what a pleasant email; I am definitely satisfied on all counts. Your letter was incredibly detailed and inspiring.

You are correct I did feel that it was time for a little taste of discipline; unfortunately I am not in a position to provide you my personal attention so I was inclined to give you a taste of what may be in store. So I wanted you to have just a taste. It appears that the taste has ignited a thirst that I am compelled and prepared to quench upon my return.

I must admit I believe I knew what the outcome of spanking your sex would be, the stinging pain of slapping your labia mixed with the sensation of having the blood rush to your swollen lips and clit must have been incredible and believe me can lead to a climax in itself. On a personal level I love the sight of this exercise and regret I was not in attendance. I particularly like administering this myself, slapping swollen labia with my hand or perhaps even a leather tongue creates a sensation that is surprising; we will experiment and practice this on many levels. I can only imagine the sensation and reaction as your labia unfolded spreading your sex and inviting more attention; yes most definitely you would beg for release.

I am also pleased that you were able to make the necessary adjustments to feel this the way I intended for you to feel it. The rush of sensations to your most private areas; the heavy breathing as you anticipate the next impact. Increasing the pace and intensity until you ache for release. You must have known that I too would appreciate this exercise with you bound and unable to move; some women prefer being blindfolded during this type of session (not knowing when the next impact will occur heightens the sensation) others prefer to watch in anticipation as my hand or the leather comes down over and over creating wave after wave of mini explosions.

***

I have asked you to prepare yourself. When I arrive, you bow your head appropriately. I ask "Are you prepared?" your response is a sensual nod, I respond with "We will see". Today I have a chain that attaches to the collar, something you have never seen; I also have wrist restraints, leg restraints and rope. The chain hangs from your collar; I run it over your stomach, between your legs splitting your labia in two. If you lean forward it is not at all uncomfortable but when standing straight up you feel the pressure of every link pressing into your already swollen clitoris.

The chain continues between your cheeks and connects to the back of your collar. I whisper to you "My dear what a beautiful sight" I connect the wrist restraints in front of you and lead you to the bed. "Lay down"; you obey. I spread you out spread eagle, your legs wide open, arms spread far apart, completely exposed to my desire. I tie your wrist and ankles to the bed post. I tell you my sweet Miselena I love the sight of a woman bearing all to me, taking all I have, and with that I reveal a slight smile. Your nipples feel the first impact of light pain; I watch your body react to my every stroke until finally I am pleased and satisfied that you have washed away all control.

I come to you tender and soft, my full lips press against yours and you can hardly believe I am the same person. You want desperately to be released to hold me, but all I give you is the warmth of a passionate, tender kiss. This is the contrast that I enjoy. To whip your most precious, tender spots, to spank your rear-end, yes loud and sometimes hard, over and over until every nerve ending in your body tingles and the blood rushes to the area that has received the brunt of my attention. I can feel your heart pounding even now. Thinking how incredibly bad this must be, but knowing that I will raise your senses to new heights. You will remember each night, each session and masturbate from the thoughts of your own wicked desires.

Most sessions will have a time for pleasure and a time for discipline; every act will be completed by a time of sensual pleasure. You will know of my pleasure, and I will reciprocate with all that you need. Most spankings will be followed by oral pleasure. Starting with my lips devouring your entire sex, taking you into my mouth, separating your labia with my tongue, sliding gently deep inside of you then retreating to soft gentle pecks. Each thrust of my tongue would be followed by a gentle sucking of your hard clitoris as if it were a miniature penis, giving the appearance of a vaginal French kiss. I can hear you moan even now as you are rocked by a series of climaxes. My tongue would creep between your legs running between your cheeks teasing your already open anus. I would instruct you to "Relax it is your time, I've had mine, and I am pleased". By now you are begging; I hear your moans and the sweet sounds that tell me you want and need release.

Today is a day of penetration. I come up from between your legs and position the chain so that I can slide the head of my penis inside you, but only to the crown, I can feel you gasp under me. I enjoy the power of knowing you want more but I will give you what I want you to have for now. Your face shows your growing impatience, and I enjoy the pleasure of anticipation. I lower my face to your breast while still inside and take your hard nipples into my mouth gently biting them careful not to penetrate deeper inside your dripping wet vagina, not just yet. Your hips are now grinding into me, forcing deeper penetration, with one look you stop this act, and I respond "Are these ropes not enough to keep you still? Or perhaps you have gotten beside yourself with pleasure and need a gentle reminder"?

I continue, sliding slowly deeper inside of you, but instead of thrusting deep into you as you desire I take your clit between my fingers and apply pressure while rotating my fingers in a circular motion. Your senses are about to go crazy; I begin my long slow thrust again, very, very slow while rotating your clitoris you look into my eyes longingly, pleading to explode. I nod to you, and in an instant your body is convulsing in the throws of a powerful orgasm.

***

If you have not noticed there are a few things I enjoy and will enjoy. I enjoy bondage and a bit of discipline. I will enjoy watching your surprise and anticipation as you do certain things for us. Yes I would enjoy watching you with another during one of our sessions, watching you masturbate in front of a stranger while being guided and protected by me.

Boundaries: You mentioned this during our IM. I want to make sure that you live your day to day life without my intervention. You will call me or we will set up our times when there is a need for us to play. I sincerely want to be the one to whom you confide your dirtiest, kinkiest, naughtiest thoughts to. I want the integrity of that to be rock solid and what I have found is this is best done if our lives are separate, as if therapy for us both! Our time will be reserved. This pleasure, this exploration is for us alone. This will be our only boundary. During the sessions there will be no limits. We will have each other in ways no one else can conceive, anal, oral and masturbation. We will please each other greatly, and when your thoughts drift during your long drives, drift to things kept only in the dark you will think of how I commanded your attention and exceeded all your expectations.

I hope that this will be a long term relationship; not one that is in the normal sense but one that will allow us both to grow and learn what it is we seek. For me I enjoy fulfilling these desires and exploring new adventures like an unopened Christmas present; each session like the closing chapter of a book so intense so engaging that all you want is to turn the page and see what excitement the next chapter will bring. This is all I want, to fulfill your curiosities, to take you to new limits, to leave you mentally and physically exhausted only to return and introduce you to some new extreme act.

Vocal: Miselena, I would enjoy hearing your moans of pleasure, your giggles, even perhaps your whimpers (if I am so inclined to spank you). Laughter is a coping mechanism for many. Our sessions will begin light, you must be comfortable. But trust me soon enough your heart will raise, your erogenous zones will throb and gentle laughter will be replaced by other more enticing sounds. You will not be allowed to speak unless previous direction has been given regarding that but you will gradually come to know what is expected of you when we begin. As you mentioned this will be a gradual exercise, and I will not take you any faster than you are willing or capable of going. Trust me it will serve neither of us to rush into some immature antics; we will proceed with care and caution but the intensity of each session is paramount to me, and I believe to you as well.

Oh the pictures before I forget. Wow, they were perfect. I was very, very, very pleased at the outcome of those and still impressed by the tan and lack of tan lines. I will have to take a few strokes off your debt for those.

Tell me Miselena, what led you to suspect you would be interested in this type of activity?

What were the circumstances (in very general terms) that led to your intimacy with another woman?

Oh interesting that you are a rider as well. We may have to explore that some day. Do you happen to have a pair of short shorts or a mini-skirt?

I think I will save the discussion of sex for tomorrow.

Good night.

November 25

Ah D,

You were pleased with my efforts. I am truly gratified, for our pleasure is paramount to this experience and I will always make every effort to return the pleasure you afford me. Earning points isn't a bad thing either, lol... how can I earn a few more...

Thank you for taking the time to assure me your guidance would be gradual yet deliberate; it is a testament to how closely you read what I write to you. I don't believe I know anyone who listens better than you. Yes, intensity is as important to me as it is you and I have no doubt that we would be intense together. What you write is intense. The feelings they engender are intense. All-in-all, this has been a very intense experience already... lol. I am going to trust you D, to take things as they seem appropriate but we really must discuss the 'other people' issues, particularly as it relates to discretion but there are other issues as well. You have said you have someone in mind... am I afforded an opportunity to discuss this with you... this subject is still rolling around in my head, unsettled. To be continued...

Having said that, yes, I completely understand that you will set the tone, the pace, the very clothes I wear or don't wear, and I will do as you wish without hesitation. Or face the consequences, lol. I am actually looking forward to it with great anticipation. I think we will be pleased with each other and that will lead to greater things.

How did I suspect I would be interested in this? This has been something of a journey. I was seeing someone who is uncannily brilliant and what I would have called then, a dominant personality. He told me I was submissive and I didn't recognize it in myself (and how could I be as old as I am and still not understand that basic part of my personality). I, being the very self sufficient person that I am, could not countenance that at all then. This all happened about two years ago and then sometime last year I picked up a copy of Exit to Eden by Anne Rampling (Anne Rice). Once I read that the analytical side kicked in. What is submissive anyway? So I started to check it out... and I am a very good research analyst... lol. I started reading everything I could get my hands on... in normal book stores and online. I was startled to recognize that I have so many traits that belong to a submissive personality, far more that I would ever have believed. When I finally accepted that I knew I had to find out more and I didn't know how; then I found AFF. That, I think, was last summer and now we are writing history; that is how new this is to me. How did you come to this and how long have you been involved? Where do you meet people (other than the obvious), or do you meet people other ways?

What were the circumstances that lead to my intimacy with another woman… well, this is a story; I have lots and lots of stories D, this one might surprise even you. It was May, and I know that date so well because it was also my wedding night. It was a beautiful wedding; the stuff of fairytales. It was a gorgeous day, all our families and friends were there and champagne and high spirits were the order of the day. That night, after most everyone had left, we got into the Jacuzzi (private suite at a Resort… I used to work there once in another life) with some friends of my husband. I have no recollection of how the subject came up but it wasn't too long before he was encouraging a night with them, beginning with a little game of pass the ice.

"Are you quite certain you want to go here?" I asked… and he said yes and was particularly interested in seeing me make love with Lisa. So, high on champagne, feeling particularly adventurous, I learned how to play pass the ice. It is a very sensuous game and Lisa has the softest lips I had ever felt. She is an absolutely beautiful woman and we all spent an unforgettable night together. And the next day was hell getting to the airport on time with all our hangovers.

Do I own a pair of short shorts or a miniskirt; yes to both and I mean both literally; my miniskirts have built-in tap pants. Tomorrow, your today, is a travel day for me. We have a half day at work and I'm off for the weekend. I am driving this week and have the company of a co-worker who also commutes. I will miss the quiet of the ride I think. I will be in touch sometime over the weekend but it will be a busy one again so I cannot say when. Please remember I always love seeing your emails, even if I don't have the time to respond right away and ah yes, I'm still waiting to hear about the sex part.

~Miselena

November 26

I think I would say most pleased at your efforts. You definitely earned points with me! We will discuss how you will work down your debt in another email.

Others are certainly an issue and we will not discuss that again until we are both ready; discretion in the lifestyle is paramount for both of us. I will require that you do certain things but none of them will cause you to be exposed to anyone other than myself (meaning your identity would be protected). You ask how I would do that, suffice to say your privacy is as important to me as my own, and I will not compromise either. Additionally, if we ever do decide to play in that fashion I will ensure we are both well protected. For now we will not discuss involvement of any outside individuals.

How did I come to where I am today? Well I discovered my talents while in a vanilla relationship. Sexually I believed my partner and I were doing all we could to satisfy each other, however after our orgasms I would feel mentally unsatisfied. I wanted more but not in a sexual way, I needed mental stimulation.

In all other aspects our relationship was great. I approached the subject with her, feeling my way mentioning as a matter of course that we could try other things but she would always respond with "I think our sex life is awesome just the way it is" even adding "my friends tell me they fake it sometimes but I never do and it is great", well that only added to my guilt. I felt a bit guilty for feeling that she was not enough.

I was in one of the yahoo groups heck I don't recall which one, and somehow I connected with a woman from Sweden and was just looking for someone to chit chat with (or so I thought). In any event we met a few times, she knew I was involved in a relationship and she was perfectly fine with that. One day one thing led to another and she asked me to drop by, I knocked and she opened the door, completely naked. Her only sentence was "What would you have me do if I were your slave"? Wow, what a powerful statement. She taught me a lot; we had sessions usually lasting a couple of hours, once maybe twice a week if it were a particularly stressful week for her. Like you she too had a job that was incredibly stressful; this was her release and soon I found mine as well.

I enjoyed the power of control, but I took care not to allow myself to lose control. She would always say we enjoyed that I maintained control and respect but we definitely took things to the extreme. Well enough of that; since then I have met a few people on AFF, but I am careful and selective. I absolutely don't enjoy playing with young women, I am just not attracted. For me it is not just the sex (yeah I know they all say that). You asked me once what do I enjoy or get out of this (a paraphrase) I get complete satisfaction. You see Miselena it is not the climax or orgasm that I enjoy it is the act leading to it. This is why I so enjoy teasing and playing and yes hearing the sounds of a woman begging for sexual release. It is traveling the road that I enjoy, and it is only a means to the final destination.

Since then I have experienced women who enjoy being slapped, spanked, whipped, bound, waxed and even written on. Yes perhaps I will explain that one some day.

Which leads me to my discussion on sex Miselena; you are extremely attractive and sex for you I imagine is no problem. I hope you agree this is not just about sex; this is about expanding our minds. Sex is not the issue exercising all; our senses are the issue for me and I hope you as well. It is almost like an incredible high; in fact one young lady (well 35 yrs old) almost fainted on me. This is why I am always so attentive to the reactions that my partner has. We will always be safe but at the same time ride that thin line so that when it is over we experience a kind of Euphoria like a runners high.

I was pleased to hear that you have minis and shorts we will put these to good uses. I will also have other things that you will wear for us, and these are items that will enhance our pleasure.

If you have an opportunity check your mail, perhaps I will \allow you to reduce your debt once again.

Miselena, do you know what a butt plug is, I imagine you could guess (and no I am not trying to be vulgar). Or have you ever experimented with leather or latex? Just curious.

November 26

Miselena,

I must admit you have fueled a hunger within me. When I read your emails, and view your pictures I entertain so many thoughts that I too am sometimes overwhelmed. I read your wedding night, and it was quite appealing. You seduced by the warmth and soft caress of a woman. Feeling her tender lips against your lips, how seductive this must have been for you all. I can imagine the moonlight glistening over you.

I am curious what other materials have you read regarding the subject of submission? Have you also investigated bondage with same vigor? What other areas have you been drawn to (perhaps things that you may not want to entertain in reality)?

Sometimes there are things that excite us because of our imagination. Watching a handsome man from across the room, perhaps a woman whose blouse is buttoned one button lower than it should be, allowing her pink nipples to show, what subtle things make you warm between your legs Miselena?

December 1

Hello D,

It feels like ages since I sat down to write and while it has only been a few days, so much about my life and my children's lives changed over this weekend. Not to mention that every muscle in my body is screaming at me. I am glad I am back this weekend for I need some time to think and refocus and I believe that is better done here.

And now I owe you answers… lots this time, but first, thank you for all the lovely compliments. I do agree this is more than sex and yes, sex is not an issue for me… or maybe actually it is and this is why I am searching. I can tell already this letter will be full of ramblings; my body is very tired and my mind seems to just take off on a whim right now. OK, I will try to focus.

Yes, I know what a butt plug is and have had some experience there; rather like them actually. I'm generally quite fond of anal play with the right preparation and genuinely enjoy orgasms with anal stimulation. Have I ever experimented with leather or latex… um… no… I'm not even sure how they might be used other than leather cuffs and whips, I mean I can certainly see more uses for leather in both toys and clothing for there is something very soft and supple about leather but latex? I can't imagine the attraction.

You mentioned warm baths… you didn't mention bubbles so let me fill that part in and tell you that is one of my favorite fantasies. Big Jacuzzi, lost of bubbles, being held to a jet, having my nipples played with… hard… kissing my neck, whispering in my ear… that's another one that would have me begging pretty quick, lol

You complimented me so highly in your last email and I thank you so much; I feel humbled actually. You have fueled a fire in me as well as I am sure you already know having done so, so skillfully and patiently. I would love to crawl inside your head and see what some of those imaginings are. And you have taken to calling me Miselena in our written sessions; that made me smile.

What other materials have I read on submission… most everything on castlerealm.com and steel-door.com among other sites, all of A N Roquelaure, the Story of O and a few more of the same genre. This particular article is what finally caught my attention in a serious way. It was sent to me by the only other person I have ever really experimented with on this level, and before we actually met: http://www.steel-door.com/High_End_Submissive.html I was amazed at both the article and the person who sent it and felt he had seen inside me, past all my barriers and all my defenses… another very intelligent man, perceptive, much like you.

Have I investigated bondage and I think this is where my naiveté emerges for I have no idea where the boundaries of submission, domination and bondage are or overlap. Virtually everything I have read has elements of both and in some cases, extreme. So I guess, having wound myself around that one, the answer is yes, I suppose I have, some anyway. How do you define bondage?

What other areas have I been drawn to but may not want to entertain… this is probably the hardest one to answer for I am drawn to most everything I have read and have entertained thoughts of myself in many of the scenarios, but as of now, I haven't let (hardly) any of it in my 'real' life, so I'm just not too sure where my own boundaries lie yet. I imagine you will be instrumental in determining some of these…

What things make me warm… hmm… this could be fun… lol… I like watching a man's lips as he talks, the same for a woman too if she has a really pretty mouth but I really like watching men. I can be turned on by just the right smile; a nice derriere on a man can be a thing of beauty, lol. Do we have to limit this to visual? I think knowing how to use the power of suggestion is totally hot; being approached from behind, standing so close I can feel the body heat, whispering in my ear and kissing my neck. A single look from across the room from the man I love. Finding I have gotten a new letter from you. Getting a phone call from a certain person and recognizing who it is before you answer. Do any of these turn you on?

I hope your day is wonderful D,

~Miselena

December 2

Well good morning my sexy Miselena.

I trust you had a great Thanksgiving even if your muscles are sore…I can only imagine the torture you endured with moving your kids; it may rival even what I will put you through ha… Me I had roasted chicken and lasagna and several glasses of a local liquor called lemon cello, after that I don't remember what else I ate. I appreciate you struggling through your exhaustion but I when I read your written thoughts I am reminded that even mentally exhausted your wit far exceed most fully awake.

Yes I have grown accustomed to calling you Miselena during our mental sessions and I believe I will continue when/if we proceed and elevate our pleasure to the physical realm. Along those lines you will refer to me with either "Sir" or "Master" when we play, suffice to say it pleases me to hear this! It will solidify the relationship we wish to establish. We will also establish a very generic vocabulary that we can use to include your safe word, and yes we will need this, (referencing your previous email). Mostly because I already see that there are some pre-conceived limits you have, I am certain that gradually we will work through the germane ones, but when we come to a point where I have the pleasure of giving you firm encouragement (read that as discipline) I want to have no doubt that you are not saying no (or hesitating) simply to further enjoy my firm hand! Together Miselena we will establish "true limits." All things short of our true limits will only cause me to take you further into those places you may have feared in the past.

Rest assured there will be no embarrassments, no shame, no guilt, and no danger only our complete release or normal day-to-day roles. It is my belief that some of your fears (but I will call them desires for our purposes) are the fuel of your curiosity, this is good. Your curiosity is the fuel we will ignite, but make no mistake I am the engine that will drive your satisfaction!

This leads me to another area. It is my intention that we will establish an objective relationship, but that being said when we have satisfied the goals of our session, there will be times of extreme intimacy. Can you maintain this objectivity? You will be directed to set the scenes I envision (no worries nothing elaborate), these may include candles, wine, incense etc…I will seductively prepare you to be mine during this time, and when our play is complete I will shower you with my pleasure. I too love a warm bath with bubbles and rest assured we will both have an opportunity to enjoy this together!

I enjoy using butt plugs; I enjoy the combination of providing pressure or light pain and simultaneous pleasure. As an example it is an incredible turn-on for me to give oral satisfaction while observing the pressure/pain of nipple clamps. As I understand it the resulting orgasm for some women is incredible with this type of action, this intense sensory overload is quite arousing for me, and this coupled with a blindfold - wow! Also something I wanted to be clear to mention I am very much aroused by the role of the submissive, in other words as you mentioned seeing a man from across the room with a certain look can arouse you sexually. I am the same way with the lifestyle. To see a woman submitting to our pleasure, perhaps her head is bowed, perhaps she is on her knees, perhaps she is displaying herself for inspection or preparation. Those actions in themselves will cause me to request your oral attention! Typically in the form of firm, clear direction!

Most direction will be short and to the point, leaving no room or tolerance for discussion. I will usually ask you to "display yourself." When I enter this will refer to you disrobing, "Your position" will refer to kneeling and "are you properly prepared for inspection" will require you to lift your arms up, hands behind your head and legs spread so that I can view your beautiful body in its entirety. If I am completely satisfied we will continue, if not...there will be a brief pause in action to correct whatever discrepancy I find.

So you ask what really turns me on...You giving yourself to me in this manner is the biggest turn-on I can experience. To watch you completely submissive, perhaps taking a sip of wine from a glass that I touch gently, softly to your lips while your arms and legs are bound, this turns me on, imagining what your voice will sound like when I call and tell you to prepare yourself, the mere thought that turns me on. Seeing your pictures and imagining what you must smell like, your skin, your sex that turns me on. Imagining what your face will look like, your expression after the last wave of control washes from your body with my mouth buried firmly into your sex while you experience your first oral orgasm with me, that thought turns me on.

Tying you up securely and running my fingertips over your body, like a soft feather, starting at your hairline, over your eyebrows, circling your lips, over your earlobes, over your shoulder blades, around your breast, over your nipples, down your hips, between your legs and stopping before meeting your swollen clit and watching you encourage me with your eyes to continue, that turns me on! You see I am not that complex at all it is the sensual art of submissive seduction, heavily flavored with BDSM that turns me on. We will share plenty, including glasses of wine.

I enjoy a warm bubbly Jacuzzi as well and it would be my pleasure to seduce you in this fashion, but this is too vanilla for us so how would I provide the twist necessary to satisfy both our desires? I will contemplate this for my next email!

Leather/Latex: Well for the very reason you mentioned leather is extremely sensual, it can be so soft and the texture heightens the erotic affect. I think I would love to see you in a collar, corset, heels and chaps. We will work on that one as they say in Italy piano, piano (slowly, slowly). As far as latex goes latex has a special feeling when used with oil on the body, it is incredible and allows for some very creative exploration.

I will share one other extreme with you this day. I do enjoy watching a woman exposed on the toilet (no nothing crazy), just the sight of a woman especially if her hands are bound behind her on the toilet in this compromising position something about that to me is highly erotic!

So what will I have you do My Pet; well I realize you must be exhausted from the previous week and it will take you a few days to recover so I will not require this one immediately. I wish for you to acquire several everyday clothes pins. I do not require you to apply them at this time however I do want you to run them over your nipples and over your clitoris (however I am not discouraging you from a little experimentation) open the clothes pins and place them over your nipples but do not close them completely, slowly close your eyes and allow your mind to drift at the thought of the pressure of one or several of these on your areolas or nipples or perhaps even your labia, this is your task ...how did it feel? Were you tempted to close them all the way? Did you? Were you tempted to masturbate?

It was great to hear from you and I can not wait to hear the results of our experiment for our pleasure.

December 2

Hi Miselena,

Wow what a holiday period, believe it or not I am still recovering! I wanted to clarify something we've touched on briefly. In your last email you asked me what my definition of bondage is. Well, I always say a picture is worth a thousand words so take a peek and tell me what your definition is... These are not all encompassing and I just did a quick look but it gives you some idea, now you show me what your definition is...

December 3

Ahhh D,

Once again you have delighted me with another experiment... you may have guessed I would enjoy this little exercise, in fact I'm betting you were counting on it... perhaps? Of course I'm referring to the clothespins and as I was searching for photos (for the bondage request) I came across many with clothespins so your comment of *several* was taken seriously. So did I try it? Yes. Did I like it? It was exquisite. How far did I go? Mmmm.... I think you would be pleased. I *was* tempted to let go entirely, did let go entirely and found that immediately the feelings would shoot from my nipples throughout my body and flood my genitals... it feels so good. And I didn't stop there (why should I when I had the inspiration of the pictures I had seen floating in my head and a whole bag of clothespins?). So I continued and added them to my labia, several actually as I found this area to be considerably less sensitive than my nipples or my breasts. Indeed D I liked it so well I have done this more than once tonight. And yes, oh yes, I was tempted to masturbate... did masturbate... it was lovely and I have you to thank for it. So thank you D, for a very sweet evening.

Now... pictures... I think? Is that what you meant by show me what my definition of bondage is? Well I have to say that you captured it most eloquently. I found a very few I

65

thought would qualify but nothing with collars. Once again I chose them for composition and beauty as much as subject matter so these are fairly mild compared to some of the photos I came across and really I think yours are more powerful.

I am having fantasies about you again D...

~Miselena

December 4

Well Miselena I certainly do hope that you wake up and find this email causes you to stir in places that will later be used for our pleasure...How has your week been? Are you finally restored after your rough weekend? What are your plans for the holidays? I regret to say my contractors have run into a bit of a snag so I have been requested to stay a bit longer, I was so looking forward to returning this month, but the work we do requires some "adult supervision" remains on site.

Now for us "My pet" how many times have I commented "perfect." Your response is precisely what I imagined it would be, and yes I knew you would enjoy or appreciate the sensation. Was this your first time with clothes pins? If it was your first did the sensation surprise you? Trust me my pet, there will be more. Things that you may have seen, that were an enigma may become quite apparent during our play. If that is the case I will be pleased but most of all I want to participate in your awareness (more to follow on that).

I am also pleased that my comment regarding several clothespins was taken serious as it should have been. During some sessions you may feel that you are covered, and all your senses on fire. I love the reaction I get when I use these, I have observed powerful orgasms using these and other forms of pressure/light pain and I so enjoy watching a woman come under these circumstances! The only thing I enjoy more is her begging to come. I am glad to here/see you say the feeling was somewhat electrifying, it is as if the pain has an express "e" ticket ride to the genitals and serves to swell and excite them! When we use these we must be careful because they can not stay on in one place too long, so I enjoy alternating locations. I love lining the labia with them, the sight is completely erotic, and seeing the labia unfold like a flower is extremely stimulating to me! I will enjoy slowly licking and gently sucking the clitoris while the clothespins are inches away from my cheek. This contrast is what I enjoy; tasting you will definitely be my pleasure. Completely aware of the pressure and pain they inflict while my gentle tongue and mouth match that intensity stroke after stroke until you explode in my mouth; yes we will certainly enjoy this pleasure together!

I so look forward to your demonstrations for I will have you perform many tasks "for our pleasure" under my observation and direction and we will call these demonstrations in my presence.

To answer your question yes I meant pictures, and I am most pleased. I particularly like the chain, and yes I have used them. If you can imagine (and I know you can) a leash connected to your collar and strung between your legs so that there is a constant pressure on your clitoris, each link splitting your labia open for our pleasure and exploration. I will admit that I did also enjoy the woman in leather, the mask excited me, it appears she is wearing a gag, very erotic... but I will admit my bias for leather is very erotic in the extreme to me.

Have you ever been gagged my pet Miselena? Oh by the way, the fact that the pictures you found were sans-collar is acceptable in this instance, of course if given the preference a collar will be preferred, and you will always be collared during our sessions... but in these cases I feel the intent of the photos are most important, so if I request you provide bondage examples with/without collar are acceptable, the same applies if I were to request clothespin examples or any other example.

You are right I have intentionally been very clear of my expectations, because I will assume any non-compliance during our sessions is a desire by you to be disciplined, and after all we are doing this for our pleasure! Occasionally, I will allow you to be vocal during a session and you will confess what things you have done that would draw my displeasure, but do not concern yourself because this indulgence will be rare...You will be silent during the core session, and we will discuss the feelings and reactions outside of that core. Oh by the way are you familiar with a riding crop?

I will take this time to also say that I will force the first session (after coffee) to be slow and meticulous, we will not rush anything! I will take my time, and appreciate your offering. What is your offering? You and I will cherish it! I want you to keep in the forefront that I am privileged to have found a submissive with your intelligence, beauty and character but make no mistake that privilege will never override my expectation of obedience.

My pet even sitting here composing this email, visualizing our most recent experiment has me completely excited and if you were here I would direct you to take me in your mouth for my penis is rigid and the tip is moist! My instructions would be clear "you have done well Miselena" and with that I would run the tip of my penis along your cheeks, spreading my fluid along your skin. I would bend down (you would be kneeling of course) run my tongue over your cheek and passionately kiss your soft lips...standing in front of you I would gently slap your cheeks with my shaft so that you could feel exactly how incredibly hard you have me and I would require a time of pleasure for myself, enjoying the fellatio that you would give me, but being careful not to release myself just yet....

Today I would like anal play and I would position you to expose yourself completely to me. You can not see what I do behind you but suddenly you feel the warm liquid oil/lubrication dripping between your cheeks, you feel the probe of my finger as I enter you, opening you, spreading you and lubricating your rectum so that my finger slides effortlessly in and out. "Perhaps this is not enough my pet?" first two, then three you feel stretched to the max but I continue I hear you whimper just a bit and I admit I enjoy it because I know you are doing your best, it appears I have finally stopped adding fingers and you relax and attempt to enjoy this feeling of being filled so completely. Finally, you hear me say "I believe you are now ready".

I can hardly wait to grab your hair for the first time and firmly place you into the positions that will satisfy our desires! To whisper commands, and to share deliverance. It will be a pleasure!

December 4

Oh by the way, yes I did masturbate vigorously with the thoughts of you following my direction dancing in my head. The sight of the clothespins as I imagine is intoxicating, I can't wait for my next task can you?

December 5

Hello D,

It is with hm... disappointment, frustration, impatience perhaps... that I respond tonight. You are not coming back this month. I don't even know what to say to that... big sigh... of course I wish you well in all that you are doing and that you will be safe wherever you are. The rest of me is not feeling so generous...

Yes, this was my first time with clothes pins and I don't know that I would say surprised as much as I would say ah damn.... and no, no riding crop or gag...

Sweet dreams... I know I need some sleep...

~M

December 5

Hello Miselena,

Trust me my pet we are both disappointed here. I had many plans and I am now hectically trying to rearrange several of them due to my current situation. I have not given up on completion but I did want to let you know the potential for delay.

The holiday is a difficult time for many, including myself. This one will be particularly challenging if I end up staying here. It seems to me that a time that is supposed to be so enjoyable is often a time of such despair. It is probably a direct result of the stress that society places on this occasion, you know happy, jolly, gift giving etc... The reality is life is often full of despair and we must endure these things because they are the true test of our mettle! It's like the saying "anyone can win with a Royal Flush, play the hand your dealt, the best you can! I can sense your somber mood, the move, work, etc... this may all be a bit disconcerting, but Miselena many would have folded with what you are accomplishing, take a moment take a breath and reflect on how accomplished and determined you are! Yes I can tell this. Perhaps you do not have a home in AZ in the physical sense but define home for me... I see many beautiful villas, even some castles but trust me my dear they are not homes, you create the home; you define the home. Do not let the physical structure be the definition, but let your presence, personality and character provide the foundation you desire! Miselena I have to tell you I believe you have an inner strength that is easily apparent and perhaps that is why I am so excited and anxious to play with you, it will come my dear, and you will be pleased that you were so patient. Thump... what was that you ask, it was my soap box being kicked out from under me...

As for me most likely if I have to stay in Europe I will be going to visit several work sites checking on work completion, we have things going on in Sicily, and the Czech Republic (Prague). Although Prague is tempting especially in the winter I had really planned on our first encounter during this time, I had so many things in mind. In fact I already had your attire picked-out (in my mind). none the less patience is a virtue I suppose. Oh I do have one question for you my pet, have you ever played in olive oil?

I believe you said you were staying in CA this weekend? Perhaps I will give you a call this holiday season, so that you can hear the voice that will whisper your commands!

Get some rest, and enjoy the peace!

December 8

Miselena,

How was your weekend my dear? Did you have an opportunity to power down and relax? I certainly hope you took a little time out for yourself, I know it's hard but we can't be much good to others if we are in need of attention ourselves.

By the way Miselena, do you enjoy going to the movies? What type of Movies do you like and what is out in the states now?

I have to admit, I really enjoyed our little pleasure Friday, you have to play hooky more often, so what else did you do besides make me desire you more than I already do. I haven't figured out if I should thank you and spank you for that. Oh hell, I think I'll spank you just for reinforcement.

You are in my thoughts Miselena and the things that we will do keep me on edge, I enjoy the feeling you give me and I continue to think of new ways to explore our pleasure. I will now share something very, very dark with you Miselena; have you ever practice controlling your flow as you go to the restroom? It is an enjoyable sight, watching a woman desire to relieve herself but doing so on command, perhaps even masturbating between releases... I know it sounds awkward but when I said control I meant control.

***

Tonight I want you to close your eyes. Think of me coming to you, and ritually placing my collar seductively around your neck. You have prepared yourself and I am pleased as I have explored every line and crevice on your body. As always I bring a bag, it is always filled with something different, even the sight of it causes you excitement. I remove your wrist restraints from my bag and attach them to your wrist; once they are secure I lead you to the bathroom - you are curious what is next.

Once inside the bathroom I string your arms above your head utilizing the shower curtain rod as support. I ask if you've had sex and you nod, I am pleased by this but you are a bit embarrassed and not quite sure how I will react. I then whisper that I must inspect what has been done to my pet and with that you willingly open your legs. Very nice I comment but it is not pink enough, with that I remove a riding crop from my bag. I can tell you are already excited waiting for what is next, but to your surprise what is next is a bottle of wine from my bag. I uncork the bottle, allow you to smell the cork, it is aromatic and fruity. I ask if you would like a sip, you nod not quite sure where this is going. I pour a glass for you and you are turned on by the sight of me serving you in this manner. I raise the glass to your lips and tilt it so that you are able to sip and enjoy this wonderful flavor.

You are amazed and turned-on that I can be so firm, so in control so strong and yet so sensual. I lick the residue from your lips trailing off to taste your neck and ear lobes, this drives you wild and I know it....would you like more... We continue in this manner, you and I sharing an intoxicating bottle of wine erotically teasing each other. You begin to feel the stir that precedes using the restroom...You know this is a period of silence and you have a dilemma how can you tell me that you have to urinate? I am keenly aware that we have shared an entire bottle and your movements and closing of your legs alerts me to the fact that you have got to go to the bathroom in the worse way.

Ahhh my dear the moment I've waited for. Would you like to relieve yourself? You nod, oh but Miselena your genitals were not sufficiently taken care of! With that I brush the leather of the riding crop over your clitoris. The only thing you can think of is urinating....but I continue to tease and hold you in place you are now very uncomfortable. With that I whisper "here my dear let me help" I lower your arms from the curtain rod and take you over to the commode, "have a seat" You are now embarrassed and are reluctant to relieve yourself in my presence. I ask "would you prefer to go back up on the rod?" You shake your head vigorously, by now you are ready to explode, you close your eyes and begin to release, suddenly you feel my pinch your nipples hard and the pain shoots instantly to your genitals, "my dear I did not give you permission" Unknowingly you have stopped and I say " now lets try this again" You begin and while you release I massage your clit, the feeling of release and stimulation is surprising and you are even more surprised at the fact that you are enjoying this....I command "stop" and you comply. "Very good", we continue, stop, go, stop, go......it is a powerful scene and one that you will soon appreciate...

***

Tonight I want you to practice stopping and starting. Visualize me there and playing with your nipples and clit while you comply with my commands for our pleasure.

D

December 8

Hello D,

How are you tonight? I am well rested; thank you for asking. I actually spent three days in bed... Friday as you well know, and which was absolutely the best day, most of Saturday and all day Sunday. It was totally decadent and exceedingly wonderful... I think a week of that on a beautiful beach with all the sexual release I can stand would be bliss.

Do I enjoy going to the movies, hm... I enjoy movies very much but almost prefer waiting until they come out on DVD. I am watching Pirates of the Caribbean tonight and enjoy almost everything except horror. There is a new Russell Crowe movie out and I hear it is excellent... Master and Commander, but I haven't seen it.

Friday was incredible D and I was so pleased by your direction and being able to follow so immediately... I am even now drifting into that lull and pull on my genitals. Mmmm... I do believe that reality will be startling in its intensity.

You are in my thoughts as well and I am pleased that you find thoughts of me exciting and enticing... I would entice you more and look forward to the time when we will face each other. Already you have taken me places I never thought of and never would have believed would be a part of my life. You have directed me along and I have willingly followed and found such pleasure in your will. You have an effect on me physically... even writing to you... reading what you have written... telling you how I feel stirs my senses and makes me warm. How I will shiver when you first run your fingers over my body... breathe in my ear... put your mouth on me... damn... *when* will you be back?

I will do your newest exercise just as soon as physically appropriate... lol... and I am doing my absolute best to keep an open mind to this one. Of course I will do exactly as you say; I am just trying to create a new association. I have to say though that I don't necessarily consider this 'dark'... dark I would more associate with extreme pain, piercing, etc. This is more frivolous I suppose... I will have to wait until the appropriate time for this (and I will push my limits on this... just for you D) to see. I am working on it as we speak with a lovely glass of Valpolicello.

Have I told you by the way, how much I adore the clothes pins on my nipples... shall I tell you? It is exquisite and yes, a direct current to my genitals. I have lovely orgasms when I use them and have become fond of them, and you are right... I do need you... I have to stop using them on my breasts as I don't know what I am doing.

When you get this you will be beginning your day... I hope it turns out to be awesome...

~Miselena

December 9

Hello Miselena,

Hmmm... three days in bed, I have to consider what that will be like; even the thought causes my mind to race. Let me fill your mind with thoughts... Our intentions are to have "sessions" 2-3hr distractions that will let me take you to incredible new limits, to explore extremes, even dark extremes if the desire so fills us.

I took notice below in your definition of dark... I think I might agree, piercing and extreme pain would be considered dark, something called fisting (you may or may not be familiar with this but it is the practice of putting your entire hand or most of it inside the genitalia) and although I am not into extreme pain, I did know a woman who enjoyed playing with safety pins. It was very interesting! You can take a safety pin and because the end is so sharp you can actually stick the nipples and feel as if your very nerve ending has been pierced, I am told this is also an electrifying feeling, but you must be careful, no piercing or penetration. It was even a turn on to run the edge of the safety pins over her nipples it would cause her to become dripping wet!

Which brings me to you....be careful with the clothes pins do not leave them on for more the 5-7 minutes, and I am not sure if you've noticed but the pain is incredible when you take them off if they have been on for a bit...what is pleasurable is gentle attention either while they are on (brushing) or gentle sucking when they come off, the same applies to the labia which I must admit would only allow me another opportunity to take your sex into my mouth. I am most pleased you enjoyed this exercise and I will guide you through others like this using clothes pins when I return, these are exercises we will share. But to answer your question yes, it turns me on greatly to hear your pleasure with the clothes pins! I even have a toy that I enjoy that is adjustable and allows you to continually apply greater pressure to the nipples, or whatever you have the clamps attached to - it is quite stimulating!

As for my return I am working steadily on that. I too am becoming anxious for our first real session, although our coffee date will create its own electricity.

When I read your statement "a week of bliss" it made me think of a fantasy I once had. In my fantasy, I arranged for a three day weekend of pleasure. Prior to our arrangement I made it quite clear that you would be kept in a submissive role the entire weekend. We

71

would have discussed this over and over, each of us making clear our expectations for the outcome but not the details of the adventure. The only thing you would know is you would serve for the entire weekend.

Initially you expressed concern and as the time grew closer I could feel your positive commitment to execute this extended session as soon as possible. I have secured a cabin, and the setting is quite soothing and tranquil. There are other occupied cabins nearby but we are alone for our intents and purposes. Before I step out of the car I ask if you are sure about this, you smile and nod. We step out of the car and immediately I take complete control! "Remove your clothes my pet". You look around to see if anyone would see your compliance and there is no one present!

Slowly you begin to strip, taking off your skirt, blouse, and bra. I place your collar around your neck and with a loud, hard swat I slap your rear end. I will continue inside, with one cool hard statement I have you "If we are to get through the weekend Miselena, your compliance must be immediate; the hesitation you displayed in removing your clothes will not be tolerated". I have gained your attention, and your ass is already pink. With that I lead you into the cabin completely naked. Your clothes are removed from the cabin and I confirm that you will not need these for the entire weekend.
"Everything you have will be provided by me".
There is a fear yet a complete acceptance that I will take care of you and you will obey. As we walk in I direct you to stand and wait for me, you simply follow my direction no hesitation, "good my pet" I leave the cabin and return with plenty of rope and a paddle that seems enormous. I run the paddle over your body as you stand there before me, running the edge over your nipples, down between your legs, splitting your labia open and then finally pressing hard into your clitoris. I find a chair that is padded and I direct you to sit, I take your arms behind the back of the chair and there I tie you up your arms tied together behind you and behind the chair, your legs are tied to the feet of the chair.

Once secure I produce a candle... today my sweet we will begin with a bit of wax... and with that, I light the candles and place them on the table waiting for the hot wax to build up for our pleasure. You see that there is a bowl and you wonder how much wax will we play with this day...You look into my face and see only a smile. Once again without a word I head for the door. You wonder where I am going but I never look back, I open the door and leave, suddenly you hear the car starting and wonder what is going on...You hear me pull off and a bit of dread comes over you... what if someone walked in - you are tied to a chair, stark naked, what could you say. You are certain I will return but none the less you are growing more anxious and concerned as each moment passes by. Ten minutes seems like hours.

I return and it seems like I've been gone for an eternity, you are frustrated and a bit upset so you choose to test the waters, you begin with "where" and the only thing you see is my smile... Almost instantly I am over to you, whisper in your ear, "the next word out of your mouth better be your safe word". In an instant you are silent. "Well my pet Miselena, since the only things exposed are your nipples and your genitals, I think today's pleasure will begin there, although you do know how I so love your ass". I remove a bag of safety pins, and my riding crop from my toy bag. What shall I do?

Unfortunately I missed you online today, we will have other opportunities I'm sure. Where will you be Friday night afternoon or night? I do not recall did we ever speak of XXX videos? Have you ever watched? If so did you enjoy or was it a waste of time? Tonight I want you to find a safety pin for me. Then I want you to close your eyes, if you have ear plugs insert them if not get somewhere as quiet as possible and run the safety pin over your nipples, around the areolas, circling then around the base running the point of the pin all the way to the tip of your nipples, follow this exercise to each nipple circling around each and slowly and ending with the pressure of the tip of the pin on the top of your nipples. Your thoughts? What other things do you consider dark?

D

December 9

Hello D,

My day is winding down and I will be heading home soon and you, I imagine are sleeping peacefully in your bed... ah... bed sounds really good right now... soon...

I have heard of fisting and yes, I would probably consider that fairly dark as well and as to what else I might consider dark? I don't know... I am not so versed in all this that my exposure offers me too many options to choose from. I do suppose spanking, crops, whips, cuffs, etc. could also be considered somewhat dark if you think about it.

As to our newest experiment; I did wait until I could wait no longer and initially the feeling of my hand on my clit while having to go so badly was extremely pleasant. I did practice stopping and starting and found that after a very few times I could no longer stand the stimulation and release at the same time. Additionally, it was difficult to completely relieve myself altogether even after I stopped touching myself. Is this common? It was almost like the one sensation short circuited the ability to function...

What would you do next with a crop and a bag of safety pins... well D, I can think of uses for the crop, but a bag of safety pins? I am afraid you will have to explain that one to me. I will do as you ask tonight with the one safety pin but I can already tell you there is nothing on the surface of that request that I find stimulating so we will see what it produces.

Friday evening I should be able to be online. I can make arrangements if you wish. I'm traveling Thursday as usual and will fly this week so the commute is a little less lengthy. Have I ever watched XXX movies... yes, I have and some are a complete waste of time and some are pretty stimulating. This is another one of those areas that is difficult to define the boundaries of arousing versus offensive although I can say that I tend to enjoy watching anal sex.

I can also say that I don't believe you would have found me so disobedient in your fantasy weekend. I think I have a pretty firm understanding of your expectations and how you feel about hesitation, as well as speaking when directed to be silent. Of course, that is easy for me to say now, isn't it, when I have yet to be tested. Let me put it this way; I don't think it will be an issue as I am turned on by the mere thoughts of your total control. And the toy you have that allows increased pressure.... yum... you keep my senses on edge...

I hope your day is wonderful D

~Miselena

December 10

It is always a pleasure to read your thoughts and share intimacies, whether dark or otherwise...

"Your experience not so versed" Then I will endeavor to provide you enough input/stimulus that you will clearly be able to determine that which is dark and that which is not.

Interesting your assessment of last night's experience. It does sometimes have the affect of canceling out both, however in the extreme and with a partner it can serve to provide a rather powerful orgasm normally occurring after urination is complete (yes dark). We will play with this more (again when I am present).

I will be quite interested to see the results of tonight's experiment; to see if the sensation stimulates you, to see if the thought stimulates you or to see if it has no bearing or relevance what so ever. We will see!

I have to agree with your taste in XXX, I too enjoy watching (well participating as well) anal sex... I also enjoy double penetration; it is very arousing to me. I will be sure to show you exactly what it looks like when you serve me anally, I will take non-descript photos of me in your ass. I will enjoy showing you exactly what it looks like, my thick shaft inside your rectum, while I stimulate your clitoris. I will enjoy watching you prepare yourself to take me there!

I do not believe I will have any concerns regarding your obedience and compliance. Although as you mentioned you have yet to be truly tested, you will be! It will be our pleasure to see the results... There will be opportunities for you to please me by baring yourself; the thought of you completely naked in the open does excite. Do not fret; nothing we do will expose either of us to any real attention, and will be done with the utmost discretion in mind although the thought of you on display does have a certain eroticism that we must explore (with limitations).

I would be pleased to meet you for IM Friday evening 9:00 pm; have a glass of wine, you may need it. Our sessions will have similar direction. After discussion regarding your specific schedules I will tell you what time is acceptable and I provide instructions for preparation (how you will present yourself to me).

I do so appreciate your emails that confirm your willingness to comply, or at least your desire... I can hardly wait to see if your heart is a big as your words, to see if you can accept the control I will have, it will be quite an experience. I will await the results of our experiment...

D

December 11

Hello D,

How has your day been? It is a travel day for me and I am anxious to be home.

Our latest experiment? Hmm, nothing, absolutely nothing, neither mentally nor physically. I wish I could say more about this but, there just isn't anything else to say.

Friday evening, 9:00 pm I will make sure I am online. And the wine will be there as requested. I have to admit I am intrigued by your comment that I may need it.

Now I have to ask you a question; we have been corresponding for quite some while and you have had a better opportunity than most to get to know the person I am that I hide so well from the rest of the world. How big do you think my heart is?

~Miselena

December 12

Miselena,

I hope your day did not become so hectic you did not have ample opportunity to absorb the beauty that surrounds you. You are right I have been through the desert and it truly is beautiful, there is so much life. You are a wonderful example of that, beneath the exterior there is so much that is undiscovered!

December 15

I believe I would enjoy a bondage fantasy with you as the central figure.
Write soon

D

December 16

***

I was nervous; the kind of anticipatory tension that precedes a monumental step and as the day wore on and 7:00 pm got closer, I was becoming more and more distracted. Four more hours, four more hours until I am truly tested for the first time.

The instructions were clear and as the hour grew closer I started to prepare myself, conscious of a desire to please and seek approval. Already my heartbeat was accelerating, my body betraying any attempt at remaining calm. The promises of seduction and introduction to submission danced through my head sending a shiver through my body and a flood of warmth to my genitals. I am thankful for the trust we have developed for this is the point when walking away is still an option and without that trust, it would be easy to do just that. But I have never taken the easy path and this time is no exception. I firm my resolve to see this through and start to dress. A very short skirt, dark blue, sheer blouse and very high heels; not at all appropriate for the weather and I am grateful for my leather coat as I walk out the door.

Downtown is not a place I frequent often and I am struck anew at the lives and bustle of the people as I park my car along the sidewalk cafes. I have left myself a block or two to walk and take deep breaths. This is it; after we meet there will be no returning. I already know I will only say yes when we are face to face. I am startled out of my reverie as the door to the entrance floats into view; I stop to stare as if it were a living thing. The tingling is everywhere now and my hands tremble as I reach for the door. Eleventh floor, I chant, end of the hallway on the right and somehow I am there. I tap, gently with my fingernails and slowly the door opens from within.

Immediately I lower my vision and bow my head in deference. A hand, strong and masculine with thick wrists extends toward me and waits calmly for my response. Warm, I thought as I gently placed my hand in his, his skin is very warm, and I was led inside. Keeping my gaze lowered I could tell we were in the hall of the dwelling and as the door closed behind me I was positioned to face the door so I could not see what lie beyond me. 'Look at me' you whisper and slowly my eyes rise, taking in the beauty of your form. Your eyes are intense and searching as they take in my face, looking for something. 'Will you step forward'? You whisper. A tremble rocks my body as I nod and take the step I have been dreaming of for months. 'Very good Miselena' you breathe as you nuzzled the side of my face and lowered your mouth to my neck. 'Remove your clothes'.

It has begun and with a deep sigh I start to remove, piece by piece, the last traces of anything that belongs to me. I feel strangely lighter as these connections to my life are left behind, calmer than before. Once I am naked and free from all the trappings of my life I stand quietly and bow my head. 'Raise your head and look at me' you breathe and as I raise my eyes, I can see your smile, soft and gentle as you return my stare. Your arms lift and I feel the collar fitted around my throat. 'You are mine now, and until you leave this place you belong to me'. I only nod. 'Close your eyes' you whisper and I feel a blindfold, soft against my skin slip into place. This serves to calm me even more and I find this to be extraordinary. I can already feel myself yielding and melting into your commands.

'Spread your legs and put your hands behind your head' you direct as you move behind me. One wrist is gently secured and I can feel a thick wrist restraint being put in place. It is padded and thick and very secure against my skin. You return that arm and secure the second on my other wrist and instruct me to place my hands behind my back. I feel you secure the restraints together and this naturally makes my back arch and my breasts stand out; too much of a temptation for you as you take one into your mouth and gently caress the nipple. Your hand surrounds my other breast firmly and you slowly apply more and more pressure to the nipple, working your mouth down my body to my genitals. Your breath on my stomach and thighs teases my skin and when you start to gently bite, the thrill of adrenaline floods my body and kicks my heartbeat into gear.

The trembling has returned and as your tongue brushes my clit for the first time, a full-on shiver racks my body as I struggle to stay still. 'Sweet' you whisper as you stand up and lavish a deep and slow kiss on my lips. My senses are totally reeling and as you sense this you slowly lead me deeper into the room.

I can sense that it is dark in the room, even though I am blindfolded and while I am only guessing, I believe there to be candles everywhere; the atmosphere simply feels this way. And there is more somehow too that I cannot quite put my finger on, something about shadows but I am distracted from my thinking as you stop my progression and unbind my wrists. Gently you rub my shoulders and down my arms until you have my wrists in your hands. I hear a gentle click and slowly feel my arms being drawn upward and over my head raising me to my toes. I am vulnerable in this position and you love it for you mean to test me today and see what makes me uncomfortable, to see what makes me conflicted with the desire to submit and the instinct to fight. Quietly I stand as I wait for you and seeing nothing but submission in me, you are pleased and lower me slightly to stand on my feet. 'Very good' you whisper as I feel you place the same kind of restraints on my ankles.

Unhooking my wrists you instruct me to kneel and take you in my mouth. It is my very first taste of you and somehow more erotic since I cannot see. 'Stop'! You hiss suddenly, grasping my hair and pulling my head back. An intense kiss crushes my lips and a thrill surges through my body at the thought that I am pleasing you. 'Bend over and lay your head on this pillow'. As I comply I can feel you securing my right wrist to the restraint on my right ankle. Then my left and I am now balanced with my behind exposed for our pleasure; totally submissive, totally yours...

~Miselena

December 17

Miselena wow, I don't think my writing can properly express the depth of my pleasure with regards to your most recent email.

Your email is extremely powerful as much in what it says, as what it doesn't say! I'll start with what it says, to my pleasure I am pleased that you understand (appears completely) the role and positions we will play during our sessions. You understand that during these times you will release your mind and body for our pleasure. I have always desired to make it clear that this is not just for me; the pleasure has to mutual and consensual. Our first few sessions will be exactly as you described them, I will test your present limits, and perhaps take you just a bit above to establish our baseline, make no mistake this baseline will just that, a "starting point" it will not be where we finish..."piano, piano" (slowly, slowly) my dear, gradually we will explore deeper than you've ever been!

We will play in places unfamiliar to you and of my choosing because just as you understand that removal of your "normal clothes", acceptance of my collar, these things will serve to wash away any semblance of your day to day existence. The environment will also be controlled by me.

I must also add very nice touch, the bowing of your head is symbolic and you understand the necessity for that show of respect and I will be honored by your desire to please, you see once again it is not all about me. It is about your giving yourself to my control. It is understanding that during our time you will have to willingly give me all that you are! I will direct you, massage you, position you, bind you, discipline you and I will be greatly aroused and pleased by your desire to submit to my will in all these things, because in the end it is about our pleasure. I will take the time and expend all the effort necessary to ensure you are safe, satisfied, and tested! This is my responsibility just as it is your role to follow my direction implicitly.

You will be directed to bow your head, kneel at my feet and show other forms of respect, submission and deference, I will taste the sweet juices that flow between your legs, my tongue will explore and tease areas previously ignored, you will satisfy me in a manner of ways but no satisfaction will be greater than the display of your obedience. I remind you that each encounter will be a test of your true persona. We will each learn a great deal about you and the true direction, nature and limits of your desire.

Did you receive my pictures?

Your thoughts on the woman in leather?

I will wait on the extreme pictures I've requested until such time as you can search in private!

What was in the shadows of your fantasy?

I enjoy lots of anal play Miselena and I do so enjoy the erotic sight of bondage and the pleasure of seeing a body held (securely) exposed with either the genitals or anus displayed for pleasure. I have seen pictures (and this is not one that I have experienced) where women are bound to the chairs that doctors use to conduct gynecological exams. Legs secured wide open, arms secure unable to move yet completely exposed! I have heard of women who fantasize about this position, even to the point of being serviced in this position. It is my belief that the eroticism of bondage is incredible in and of itself. Whether it is a mask, ropes, restraints, collars, corsets the symbolism, apparel and positions create a world that is intoxicating. I will have you displayed in this manner and we will satisfy one another for our pleasure.

D

December 17

Ahhh... you were pleased; that makes me smile.

I did receive your pictures yes, and other than the fact that she is very beautiful it really didn't stir any feelings one way or another. The wrist bar reminds me of the movie The Secretary; have you seen it? I have attached a few of the extreme clothespins shots we discussed the other night; this is what I was supposed to get, right? I had a few glasses of wine that night and some points are a bit fuzzy if you know what I mean.

What was in the shadows of my fantasy? Ah ha! You are so good and listen so well, lol. I put that in there specifically for you; to *allude* to a presence of others as opposed to *acknowledge* a presence of others. Did you like it? I was smiling as I wrote that part; I'm smiling even now, that sentence was fun to write. This correspondence has been an exceptional exercise in writing skills and I find I really enjoy it. I think I could do even better if I had more time to devote and perhaps I will start to set aside time now that I am staying in CA more. I was hoping you would pick up on it and you did. Very cool.

I am off to bed now and wish you a beautiful day,

~M

December 19

Miselena,

So tell me what about this Secretary movie? No, I don't believe I've seen it. Is it similar to 9 1/2 Weeks, the Mickey Rourke movie that aroused the layman's fantasies? Tell me just a bit about it when you have a chance perhaps I will try and find the DVD.

Oh the pictures did not stir an interest, well I have to admit, and there is more behind the pictures that I send than just the immediate arousal. Even now I am testing your tolerance and like the safety pins things that you find generic or vanilla may take on an entirely new meaning once we exercise my applications. It is your tolerance I seek (for now!).

Yes I loved your story, there are a couple of positions in bondage that I find arousing, erotic, sensual and to be down right blunt, hot! One of the positions you mentioned, where the submissive's rear is completely exposed even symbolically offered to the dominant, the other position is one that I described where the submissive is in a sort of chair, bound to the chair with her genitals in a similar presentation (offered). You will become familiar with both.

It was also a pleasure to see that the thought of an onlooker, has not been abandoned in your fantasies. The thought of you displaying yourself, offering yourself to me, complete and uninhibited is exciting in and of itself, but the thought of you presenting yourself for me while the entire scene is observed by a third party, perhaps not a physical participant but an observer is very, very arousing! We will explore this at another level. In my mind the thought of someone watching this display, your beauty, and elegance void of any personal control but giving to me and knowing that somewhere in the shadows I can just make out someone masturbating while they watch you obey my every instruction. It is a thought that even now causes my genitals to swell with incredible desire.

We will please each other in so many ways and those things that you could not accomplish on your own will be achieved through our mutual perseverance and desire. Like you I am incredibly anxious to begin our journey for our mutual pleasure. We will soon come to the intersection where stories will not be the center of our passion but the memory of our actions will fuel increasing desires. What I have found in the past is the pleasure achieved during the session drive a self-sustaining mechanism that will fuel ever increasing limits and test, I will ask you each time are you prepared and each time you must respond "I am ready and willing" after that the only detour available will be your word and I will be honest I can hardly wait to present you with this option!

D

December 22

Ahhh D,

I am sick, sick, sick and need a hot toddy, a pillow and a blanket, in that order. Most of this weekend was spent in bed nursing this cold and it is still hanging on. How long do colds last? I haven't had one in forever and sure wish I didn't have it now. Oh well...

I *was* tired the other night; I am generally in bed, *asleep* by 9:30 or so because my days start so early. So, anything past midnight has a fair shot of being lost on me. It is the strangest thing really; my body will just quit and fall asleep. I have been known to fall asleep in the middle of parties, right there on the couch with the noise all around me, completely out (not alcohol induced). And I think I do need more sleep than the average person. I have a friend who can't believe I actually sleep 8 hours a night; I think he sleeps like five and I can't understand how he can function on that. Anyway, I am rambling because I am sick and fuzzy headed.

The Secretary, with James Spader is a *very* good movie and you should definitely go out of your way to find it. I don't want to say more because I don't want you to have any preconceived notions and I would love to hear what you think of it. It is nothing like 9 1/2 Weeks and did you know there is a sequel called Another 9 1/2 Weeks?

Testing my tolerances, are you? Hmmm... You must surely have a great deal of knowledge amassed so far; you are so good at this after all. I truly have never corresponded with anyone who paid such close attention to my every word. It is a lovely compliment and I thank you. I am curious if you have formed an opinion yet, of whom I am and how I work, good and bad.

Wow D... even now, feeling as sick as I do, I re-read you letter and I get hot. Amazing. For two months now you have kept me enthralled with your letters. I wouldn't have believed it possible but there it is; incredible. I know you like the idea of an audience. The timing for this was weird actually because just prior to your request for a fantasy, one of the men I am dating expressed an interest in watching me make love with another man. Note I said 'make love' as opposed to 'view a session', for he has no idea of the depth of my interest in this. So... it wound up in my fantasy and I knew you would pick it out; indeed, you have pounced on it, lol... I am delighted.

I hope you have an awesome day D,

~Miselena

December 23

Miselena, first I am so sorry to hear that you are not feeling well. Nyquil is great and so is Thera-flu, they usually work well for me however they make me incredibly drowsy and like your other friend I usually do well with 5-6 hrs a night. How long do they last? Well depends on how much sleep you get, so yours should be over very, very soon ha, ha, ha... just teasing. Just stay warm and drink plenty of fluids.

I will make every effort to secure this movie The Secretary. I am now officially curious and no I didn't know there was a sequel to 9 1/2 weeks, very interesting!

My thoughts on you are varied. I am incredibly turned on by your intelligence, maturity and free will. I enjoy the fact that you know where you want to go, just not sure how to get there yet. I enjoy being the transportation for the ride you are about to take. It's kind of like taking your friend on your favorite roller coaster, you've ridden 100 times, you know exactly where it dips and curves and you take special pleasure watching your friend's enjoyment even shock as they experience the ride with you. I believe you are just what you alluded to in a previous email, a sophisticated sub, a submissive with class but a sub none the less, and I will treat you respectfully but, as a sub. My impression is there are many things that you are curious about, even things that may not attract you (yet) but that you observe and wonder if there is an attraction that you do not perceive.

I will be perfectly honest, I will test you in every way, you will come to clearly define and understand that which is vulgar, and that which is not. I know that the thought of an audience for you has a certain excitement (just my opinion) but that discretion and safety are paramount (understandable and right on all counts). I know that you want to try so much, but freely, never completely giving yourself up. This is our challenge and I say our challenge because you share my desire to have your will. As much as you want to give in there is something that forces you to hold on. Our goal will be complete satisfaction for us both. There will be things that you do that you will want to contemplate that will last for a bit but ultimately we both know your desire. Among other things you will have an audience for me; however you must know that the beauty of what we will have/do will be without judgment and no guilt, this is often times difficult when we include someone significant (a boyfriend or girlfriend) and that is why I will demand objectivity. You will know that I care for your safety, our pleasure, our satisfaction but at the end of the day, I want you to return to your normal life. I want to be the dark secret that you retain, one that gives you those things that no one else can, one that can satisfy your lust for submission. You will give me much in terms of satisfaction; your compliance and obedience will satisfy my lust. It is a relationship but it will be not be conventional.

I have to tell you I find it very exciting that your friend has expressed a desire to watch you with another; maybe he has dominant tendencies himself or better yet maybe he is a cuckold? Has he shown any jealousy? Is he aware of your submissive desires? He wants to observe you make love to another; maybe he wants to see the sensual side of your passion from the other side, you must be incredible in bed.

I do not share his desire. I do not want to observe you making love, I want to observe your ability to comply and obey and if that means jacking off someone else, while blindfolded and listening to my every command, could you comply? Perhaps we will see.

I hope you feel better; we will suspend any direction until you are a bit better.

Get well soon; I have many things for you to try my dear.

D

December 23

Five or six hours of sleep a night. I cannot fathom how you function on such little sleep; wish I could do that. I am feeling better today and am already in bed for the night. I plan to read myself to sleep early; tomorrow is a travel day and it starts bright and early at 5:30 am. I've been doing all the meds and while I am still a bit fuzzy, I think I am on the mend.

Your thoughts are accurate as usual; lol... all of them, including the 'challenge' one and I particularly liked your roller coaster analogy. I appreciate your thinking on judgment and guilt and understand that exposure to a significant relationship could have lasting impact.

My friend has never been married so he cannot have been cuckold and I think he may have some dominant tenancies but he is holding back, and for some reason I think he is holding back with *me* and might not necessarily with someone else. I don't really know him well enough yet. He *is* aware that I have submissive desires and has spanked me a few times, but again, I sense he is holding back. There could be a lot of reasons for that though; it could be that he doesn't feel that he knows me well enough yet, I don't know. And no, never has there been any display of jealousy; quite the opposite in fact. He wants all the details of my relationships with other men and asks explicit questions. It excites him, no doubt. It was after just such an inquisition that he asked if I would allow him to watch me with someone else.

Perhaps we will see? I have no doubt we will see just how far I can go; that is of course if you ever get back to the United States, lol. Are you lonely over there? I am sorry you have to be away from family during the Holidays and do hope you have some peace from the season. God Bless you D, and Merry Christmas.

~Miselena

December 24

Good morning Miselena,

If you read this before you start your day I wish you safe travel and wonderful weather. I realize you have a big day and traveling can be a bit tiring as well. You mentioned that you are beginning to feel better, I certainly hope so. I will send you a nice email on the 26th you mentioned quite a few things in this one and I want to respond and comment on them.

Oh by the way yes I do get lonely at times but I am always able to find a friend to satisfy any need for companionship. Take care my dear.

D

December 26

Miselena,

I can finally take a breather and give your emails the attention they deserve. I've been a bit on the run lately sending members of my crew back on leave while attempting to maintain a semblance of productivity throughout the entire holiday season. So as you can imagine my early days are more than anything a habit I formed long ago and now it's like second nature. For me getting up at 7:00 is a late day. I am not hyper by any stretch however if I sit still too long I begin to think of all the things I could be doing and how I could be doing them if I weren't lounging. Even now I am making preps to visit the Czech Republic (Prague). More work than anything, I'll probably freeze my buns off. I'm told it's incredibly cold there this time of year; we'll see.

I am pleased that you understand my take on objectivity. I have seen women and men do things to satisfy their lovers only later to have them regurgitated in some obscene fashion. I have seen the look; the look of embarrassment when a woman does something and then wonders if I think differently of her because she was completely free with her desire and lust. Those individuals do not understand! It is the ultimate gift to give completely but it is not for everyone. If the guilt of what you do overrides the pleasure you receive, it is simple, don't do it! I once had a sub that loved being a sub, she would call and ask me for sessions but later she will feel guilt; guilt at her performance, not because of my response but because she wanted so bad to conform to what society said she should be. She was extreme, her desire and lust would take over and she would call but ultimately the conflict within her caused me to discontinue our sessions. Miselena; to truly appreciate your lust and desire you have to step outside the norm. This is what draws me to you. There are many submissive women however there is something exceptionally arousing about a submissive with the class, education, and desire that you have.

I have to share this with you; I once had friends, a married couple that enjoyed an open relationship. The man knew his wife was attracted to me, and apparently she had asked if he would mind if we had a bit of fun, he asked if I would play with her while he was on a business trip but he wanted to listen in on their speaker phone.

I would have never done this with anyone else however I knew these two quite well. In any event I had his wife on speaker phone, we had straight explicit sex and she conveyed everything that I was doing to her, and how it felt different but apparently he enjoyed because we could tell he masturbated through a good portion of it. Let me ask Miselena does it make it especially sweet or bad or exciting to have this alternative persona? To give a glimpse of your desires to someone but knowing inside that they don't know the true depth of your potential. To have someone to satisfy your normal emotional needs and physical needs, but for those elevated extremes to have someone to take you to your absolute limit emotionally and physically. Does that arouse or excite you, or have you ever given it any thought?

Now for us.

Isn't it ironic that we have discovered each other at a time when physically we remain separated. It is the ultimate tease! I do so enjoy a good tease but this is ridiculous.

Miselena, I have taken you over and over in my mind. I have gagged you, blindfolded you, tied you to numerous posts, chairs and beds all in my mind, but no vision is as powerful as those I have where you present your ass for our pleasure. It is particularly arousing to me to have you present yourself of your own free will; to display your body for my inspection and then to prepare yourself to satisfy our desires. In my thoughts I call you and schedule a session for you, but this time we will be mobile. You are a bit concerned and although you want details you know it is futile to ask and even greater than that your sense of curiosity as to where this will lead outweighs any other concerns (we have built a nice trust).

***

I tell you to be in heels and I will pick you up. Now your concern is elevated; I've always told you exactly what to wear but if we are traveling in a car you can not possibly travel in heels alone (what if someone sees you).

Wisely you ask no questions and prepare yourself as directed. When I arrive you are in heels.

You are required to present yourself to me; you bow your head, and spread your legs wide spreading your genitals for me to inspect and taste. Are you ready? You nod, then let it begin; I place the collar around your neck. My face is inches from your own and you feel my hot breath against your skin as I slowly lower myself. I am very careful slowly smelling you, but even more than that breathing softly against your skin, down your neck, over your breast and nipples until finally I kneel between your legs critically scrutinizing every inch of your genitals. Today I am especially pleased so I linger tasting your sex as if it quenches my dying thirst. You love the passion with which I perform cunnilingus and you want me to continue releasing the moans of your first orgasm, but it can not be that easy.

I am very aware of your legs vibrating under my steady tongue. I raise my head and grab your hair at the very roots pulling your head back and allowing you to taste your sex from my lips. I turn you around and whisper in your ear very firm "continue". Your hair still clenched firmly in my closed fist, but now you are facing away from me and I have full view of your tight ass. I force your head down so that you can bend over and present your ass for my scan and potential probe. I run my tongue over each cheek and unexpectedly slap your firm ass several times until I feel each cheek warm from this painful attention. Again I run my tongue over your cheeks, "ah Miselena much better. The warmth of your spanking makes your skin taste so sweet".

My tongue follows the seam of your ass rimming and teasing your tight entrance, gently probing, testing your conviction. "My dear I do believe that you have not completely released yourself to me, I sense a bit of tension" Again, I slap your ass one, two, three, four, each strike harder than the last until you are tender and your sense of control washed aside.

I pull your head back once again, and I see the sparkle of a tear in the corner, affectionately I lick the tear from your eye and whisper "during our time there is much to endure" I continue sliding down to taste your sex once again, stopping at your ass and feeling a sense of relaxation that was not present before. "Very good my dear, you taste delicious."

I brought a long button down coat and I instruct you to put it on but leave the bottom 3 buttons undone, "it is evening my dear and I wouldn't want you to catch a cold" I say as I smile. I inform you that I am going to my car; you must wait 5 minutes then come out to the car and wait at the passenger door.

You follow my instructions to the letter, as you walk to the car you notice I am on the phone and that I quickly hang up but have an interesting smile on my face. You wait at the door and I come around to open it, you also notice that on the seat is a black hood and a pair of balls that have a remote control on them. I hand you the hood and instruct you to hold it. I lubricate the balls with lubricant from my glove box and instruct you to squat (now you know why I instructed you to leave the last few buttons undone), without hesitation you oblige. I slide one ball in your vagina and the other in your anus. "You may stand" I hand you the control for the time being and tell you to get in. Again you obey.

I enter on the drivers side and once the car is started tell you "The controller my dear", you hand me the controls and I test the operation of our toy, our little joy ride has begun, but the question remains what will we do with the hood.

***

Miselena, once you are completely well, I want you to find a pair of latex gloves (can be found at any Rite-Aide or grocery store) I want you to set a scene for me, soft music (yes enigma is great) perhaps a candle. Get olive oil and pour enough on your body for your nipples and genitals to be well lubricated (saturated). I want you to put the gloves on and masturbate, think of your friend watching me have you or you following my every command while others long for your touch, think of how sensual you are and how incredibly erotic your body is, wear the latex gloves Miselena and masturbate.

Tell me the results.

Happy Holidays my dear and perhaps we will give each other something very, very special this coming year, satisfaction.

D

December 29

Hello D

Oh do I understand taking a breather. I feel the same way and life (work) just got busier. January is going to go by in a blur if everything that is slated to be done actually gets done. I had to smile at one of your comments (well more than one but this one in particular) about sitting too long. I have long maintained that I don't 'sit' well so I can totally relate. So are you in Prague yet and is it very cold? It has been unusually cold here, way too cold for my blood.

I meant to do your next task when I got home but I was exhausted from the day (up at 5:00 to hit the road in time to catch the game). So tonight D, I will comply with this new, (where are you going with this?) task... lol.

Yes I am on the mend and for all practical purposes, over it; thank you for asking, and very happy to be so. I have to ask you a question about the 'interesting' comment you made on the cuckold issue; why would that have made it interesting? I ask because someone else I date was cuckold and has some subsequent issues.

My alternative persona. Now that is an interesting subject and one that has been in sharp relief since my taking a job in CA and essentially living two lives with two complete casts of characters. This has been such a strange time in my life and not like any I have ever lived before. As to my sexual persona, lol, I have a friend who calls what he knows of that side of me to be Mistress Elena and says I have two very distinct personalities. Guess which one is more fun, lol.

Is it exciting? It is the adventure that is exciting more than anything, and pushing my limits where no one else will dare push me. I get that at work now but it isn't enough or totally of the energy I wish to explore. It arouses me immensely to think of you controlling and testing my limits, pushing me to complete release. Totally. This *is* the ultimate tease, lol.

I loved your story (I always love your stories) and can't wait to get them. Someday D. someday will we meet do you suppose; what a trip that will be. I am off to your task. have an awesome day,

~Miselena

January 4

Miselena, my Christmas was nice; a girlfriend actually came to visit me so it was quite nice. I can relate to the dual personas because she has no interest in submissive or dominant activities and so I restrain myself intensely when I am with her. I have truly come to need the release of my dominance to function properly day to day. It is very interesting I do not need or require consistent release in this manner however if I do not have this release I am affected in other areas of my life mainly the stress of work. So when I said I need this as much as you I was completely honest, it is not necessary that I have this release day to day (every day) but I have come to accept and appreciate that this release helps me in so many ways.

Prague was awesome, the food was great and they have appeared to embrace capitalism with open arms. I even had sushi. I had an extra special treat as it snowed during my visit and where I am in Italy I seldom get any so that was nice during the Christmas season.

Again, I wish I would have contacted you prior to my departure. I left on the 27th, I had a rather lengthy layover in Zurich and I spent much of it thinking of compromising positions (physical positions) to place you in. Soon you will see how special this is.

As for the cuckold statement, I was being sarcastic. Although it would have made it interesting, my experience in that area is extremely limited. As I understand it the cuckold gets off on giving his wife to another, in fact encourages her sexual relations with others, even subjugating himself to her pleasure with the "others". It appears you have more experience and information in this area. I am curious of your experience and the results you've witnessed. Expound on this. Issues? Oh and the reason why I said interesting, if this "friend" displayed this behavior he would take pleasure in giving you to others and being submissive during the setting, submissive to the point of cleaning you prepping you etc...Just sounds interesting and has some potential.

Will we meet? You have got to be joking; can we do anything but meet in person now? Our mutual desires have drawn us together like two magnets polarized for attraction (+ and -). Yes, yes we will meet and I am trying to solidify a time to return even if I have to come back for just a bit, I want to initiate you! I want to give you a physical taste. A taste of your true potential and the satisfaction you can have by giving what you hold most cherished: "control". Yes, we will meet; soon, very soon we will talk on the phone and ultimately without a doubt, we will share sessions that I will dominate and you will appreciate.

Miselena, did you complete the task as assigned? What were the results?

Do not forget to amplify your cuckold experience.

Soon my dear, very soon!

D

January 4

Hello D,

It is lovely to hear you may be back in the States soon; it is something I am looking forward to with both anticipation and trepidation, lol. I am going to be online tonight at 9:00 pm but I do have to leave off early as my Monday always starts at about 5:00. It is my busy day for reporting and meetings and I have to be on my toes.

I am so glad you had company over Christmas; I did not like thinking you were alone. And now you are back in Italy? You world traveler; how *was* the sushi in Prague? And was the restaurant crowded? And you saw snow; I haven't seen snow fall in years. There is something magical about standing out in the snow when it is falling gently all about you. Hm, I may have to go somewhere I can see the snow this winter.

I cannot tell you how pleasing it was to hear you think about me and visualize being together. I can only imagine from here, and fantasize, which I do. Yes, by the way, I did your task and enjoyed it very well. I lit the candles and turned off the lights, I do so love candlelight. I think I'll light some now, there; that is better. It is very seductive in here right now. I wonder if we will connect tonight. Anyway, back to the olive oil, it felt so smooth gliding my hands over my body and the gloves were a little different but it was nice. I used a lot of oil so it was very slippery and I think if it had been the skin of my hands instead of the gloves that it would not have felt quite so slick. It was so sensuous running my hands down my thighs and up over my breasts trying to pinch my nipples and having them slip through my fingers; sliding my fingers down, over my ribs and stomach, gliding because there is no friction, slipping into my vagina and back up to caress my clit, imagining all the while you there, whispering in my ear. "Slap it Miselena, now, harder, yes baby, caress it, mmmm... give me your other hand. I want you to slip a finger in your anus, yes, does that feel good? Shhh... Now another..." My breathing is so ragged and aches for release, throbbing yet floating at the same time. The release was exquisite and intense and draining. And my skin loved the oil and was very soft as a lovely after effect. Thank you. That was a lovely experience and one I totally didn't expect to enjoy so thoroughly. Are you pleased?

Cuckold... is a very involuntary position in the definition of the word, and an extremely abhorrent one for most men; an insulting one and generally very hurtful as it is a betrayal of trust. So, I am not certain it is the word to describe that of which you speak; perhaps voyeur.

And you speak of initiations and initiation is just what it would be. I don't think I would trust any other person with what we propose, and that I feel I can trust you speaks volumes for you D. I hope we connect tonight,

~Miselena

January 5

Miselena,

Like you the first week of the New Year is incredibly hectic especially after returning from a road trip. I checked my mail this morning and unfortunately I misread your email (when I took a quick glance). I read that you would be getting in bed very early and therefore would not have an opportunity to chat, perhaps it was my haste I would prefer to believe it was my labored breathing as I read your story and enjoyed your experience, which will be our experience! Now that I am on that subject I did so enjoy the brief summary you provided me regarding your oil experience. You are absolutely right the texture of the oil against your body coupled with the latex provides a very interesting and erotic combination. Even the thought of pouring oil over your body and then directing what your experiences were in this area is arousing.

I love Enigma, their music is very unique. Anyway it can definitely set the right tone/mood. I imagine the candles with the light of the flame flickering against the walls casting beautiful images of your incredible body. The music adding to the ambiance of this your masturbation while I watch with eager anticipation has my penis engorged and ready to explode, yes seriously.

As for the cuckold then perhaps there are several interpretations of this type of relationship, however anything which has a lasting negative affect does not interest me in the least. However I have heard men call themselves cuckolds and actually offer their wives, girlfriends etc. for the pleasure of others; perhaps the negative part is that in reality the female is dictating this behavior not at the behest of the husband or partner but in spite of the partner. Anyway as I said it was just an interesting diversion. Only matched by the outline of your body, your nipples erect and swollen, your breast natural and full and finally the outline of your shapely ass. I am so pleased you enjoy anal play as much as I. I will take immense pleasure in penetrating, teasing, and playing with that tight ass of yours!

Since this week appears to be a bit of a challenge for both of us, perhaps we would stand a better chance shooting for a phone date towards the end of the week. I wish to command you verbally; I want you to hear my voice and respond in kind. Perhaps if we plan far enough in advance we can accomplish this with minimal diversion. What about Friday night, where will you be? And can you be reached by phone? Or would Sunday night work better for you?

Now for our pleasure Miselena, in my mind I see you covered in this oil your body glistening, shimmering from the sheen the oil has provided. Since we both enjoy anal play so intensely I would enjoy placing your fingers in your tight anus 1, 2, even perhaps 3 fingers, carefully observing your facial expressions while I perform cunnilingus on you tasting the sweet juices of your climax. But that would be like placing the cart before the horse as it were. I would first encourage your obedience as you kneel in front of me, feeling your warm tongue and mouth engulfing my shaved shaft and testicles. My testicles like miniature footballs in your mouth; you release them running your tongue the length of my shaft, finally covering the crown of my penis with your soft lips. Perhaps your mouth would be stretched by the girth of my penis, perhaps you would gag a little but I would continue to encourage you to take it all for our pleasure.

When I am satisfied that you truly have taken all that you can swallow I will pull your head by the roots of your hair and dislodge my penis from your eager lips praising the job that you did to satisfy me so intently. Your reward will be tonight only 5 swats on your ass instead of 10. I instruct you to assume a decent spanking position (all fours) and before we begin I would spread your cheeks wide open teasing your anal opening and the entrance to your wet vaginal passage. Of course I would linger here until I had you on the brink of your first climax and stop abruptly just short of your own satisfaction. A little more attention my dear.

The first smack is very, very hard; the speed and intensity of the impact stings but even greater is the surprise. You were not expecting this one and it is the surprise that brings the excitement and lubrication immediately over your labia. My whispers are so warming and sound sensual; you enjoy them so much during our sessions and I know to provide you constant auditory stimulation pleases us both. I tell you how incredibly special you are and how lucky I am to have a submissive so obedient and eager. Are you Miselena? Are you eager to obey? You nod. Good!

"Turn over". When you do you see many clothes pins on the table. Tonight my pet we will see how eager you are to obey and if you are good submissive. I will fill your ass until you cum screaming with pleasure. But first we must have your genitals tender and ready for our pleasure. I display to you a riding crop. I slap your clit and labia. The initial impact causes blood to rush to your genitals and you want to let out a whimper but you know only a minimal amount of noise will be tolerated. Again, slap! Oh, this one lands squarely on your labia and they are quickly becoming a nice rosy color. I hand the crop to you, "hold this" and gently, softly I take your labia into my mouth, soothing the sting with the warmth of my mouth and the silky strokes of my wet tongue. Now it is your turn Miselena, do not disappoint me!

January 5

Hello D,

I told someone about you today and about our conversations and where this was all going. Someone I trust with my life and probably the only person with whom I will share this. He was surprisingly open to the idea and only concerned for my safety and the fact that you are a stranger to me. I think what was most surprising was that he has been having some of the same thoughts and desires with his wife in the past few months, hence a lack of disapproval or disappointment in me. It was a revelation and felt very good to talk to someone.

As far as talking; Sunday would be better for me as long as it isn't too late. What time did you have in mind? Let me know and I will plan to be home and available. And ping pong paddles? I only bought one.

And then you say "now it is your turn, do not disappoint me..." I must be having a blonde moment D. what is it my turn to do? It is the (almost) end of a long day and I still have one more battle to fight before my day is through. I must be brain dead but I cannot afford to be tonight. I am sorry. I hope there wasn't a task in there for me that I am just too fuzzy to see.

I will write more as soon as I can. I think it is time for me to write you another fantasy.

~Miselena

January 7

Good Morning Miselena,

Desire is really not all that uncommon. The strength to experience your desires however is uncommon and I can tell the strength of your character by the strength you have to carry out and see just where your desires will take you.

No task last email "your turn not to disappoint" was just an extension of the fantasy.
Sunday will work fine I will give you a time and how to prepare.
Now, for you, yes it is time for a fantasy from you!
D

January 7

Oh Miselena,

I almost forgot. This week has been hell. New Year and all (appears you are equally exhausted). I do not want you to feel I have lost interest in the least; it is just taking me a bit longer than I expected to catch up from my trip to Prague. I hope all is well with you and your family and that you get a decent amount of rest and that both our lives slow down just a bit so that we can enjoy a bit of mutual decadence.

I did have a question; does your friend (the one you shared our conversations with) know the extent of your submissive desires, and have you ever been intimate with him? Just curious.

January 9

Miselena

Between 7:30pm and 8:00 pm Sunday would work best. We will begin with IM and if I am pleased I will call.

D

January 11

Hello D,

You must think I have fallen off the face of the earth and socially I have. Twelve hour work days and weekends are doing me in and cutting into your time as my systems conversion is (I think) finally coming to a head. It is going to be this way until mid February but I will do and write as much as I can in the meantime.

You haven't forwarded too many questions in your last few emails so this will be brief. Yes, my friend (confidant) does know the depths of my desires and yes, we have been intimate, but that was years ago. Today we are just very close friends.

I owe you a fantasy and God only knows when I will have the time and energy to devote to it, but will find it, I promise. I will be online per your request (IM will say I am not but I will be) and look forward to hearing from you. Now I am going to try to get a little rest.

Ciao,

~Miselena

January 12

Miselena,

You continue to amaze and astound, in a good way of course. This morning (my morning your evening) I called with the specific intention to test to see if you would be in shock by my demands or if you would be amenable. You continue to show that your submissive desires are not some casual thought. You showed me that you are serious about bringing your desires and your fantasies to fruition. I jumped directly into a phone session not out of enthusiasm but to test your resolve once again, and once again you have satisfied me in ways you can't imagine (at least not yet). As I spoke to you over the phone I saw your compliance, I saw you lying there obeying my wishes. Towards the end I sensed a combination of surprise and relief. I could almost sense you were becoming amused by your own response (even perhaps a chuckle). Let me assure you no truer words have you spoken, it will be much different/better in person but you did meet all my expectations as I hope I yours. The one thing I found amusing was as I sat there with my eyes closed thinking of your body and how it might look in the position I had you in. I lost complete track of time and what was suppose to be a brief tease quickly extended to nice fantasy. You are right this was not the real thing, and when the real thing occurs we will not be encumbered and I will slowly, slowly take you to a place I am convinced we both want to explore. Thank you for giving yourself, but the best is yet to come.

Now tell me your thoughts, did you find humor in our shared task? We you surprised? Were you relaxed and able to drift into a real sense of pleasure?

Waiting for your fantasy and counting the spankings I will give you for your delay

D

January 12

And you my friend are brutal; you want both my reaction and my fantasy on pain of reprisal. Did I mention that I'm working 12 hour days and weekends lately? My day today (eighth day in a row) started at 5:30 and I have just quit working (it's about 7:00 now). And I do not know you well enough yet to know if you would prefer anything (something is better than nothing) or if you would prefer to wait for me to have an opportunity to address the subject properly (a poor effort is no effort and therefore punishable as well). What to do; I will give you my best effort D and apologize up front for a certain quality that may be missing.

Your call, that was nice. It was nice to hear your voice especially and yes, I was surprised and delighted (humor - delight - semantics really). It was distracting though to have to hold the phone and I kept drifting in and out of imagining you were right there; that was distracting too. So while I enjoyed it I think it will pale by comparison. I was really caught off guard when you asked me to tell you about the oil. Why is it I wonder that it is so much easier to write than to speak? Thank you for allowing me to bow out of that quickly. And as to your testing my conviction, you sound almost surprised. Your emails have been quite explicit. If I had been shocked by anything you said it would have been to my discredit for you have been quite clear in your expectations. What did you really expect to happen I wonder? You amaze me that you can be so focused and put voice to your thoughts so clearly and fluidly; you went beyond my expectations D.

***

It was raining. That, in of itself was nothing new; it had been raining steadily for days, a soft, persistent curtain on the city. And the air smelled fresher, the rain having washed away the layer of grime that can settle in every nook and cranny. I watched it ping the puddles in the street as I walked down the sidewalk. I was on my way to yoga and consciously trying to clear my mind... slow down... take slower, deeper breaths... relax... and not bump into the people on the sidewalk. The rain doesn't keep people off the streets in New Orleans; these people are ducks.

I quickly ducked into the building and changed into cotton, calf length tights and a fitted crop top. This was Bikram yoga and the room is heated so you sweat. A lot. And your body temperature rises the longer you are in there. I took a seat in the back with my knees bent and my arms draped over them, hanging my head. Relax... clear your mind... and the room fades and the sounds fade. I don't know how long I was there; you lose time when you fade out like that but the next thing I knew we were being called to stand and when I raised my head and saw him I couldn't breathe. Immediately my skin began to tingle as if a million nerve endings snapped their fingers to attention and a warm flush settled in my genitals. "Stand up!" I silently shouted to my self and began to unwind from the floor. My heart was positively pounding and as I stood I started chuckling in a wry, self-deprecating sort of way. This had to be Karma.

Ahsan stood in the front of the room slowly taking in the size of the class, noting who was there and I had a minute to watch him before he saw that I was there. I think I must have been holding my breath, waiting. And there it was. And it was good. His eyes lit up and his mouth betrayed a controlled attempt not to smile too widely. It made him utterly charming and my heart skipped a beat. Ahsan is gorgeous you understand. His name means act of kindness and his personality mirrors that so his physical beauty is merely the icing on a truly beautiful man. He has long, dark hair and eyes so brown as to be fathomless; just looking at him was enough to make breathing difficult.

I started laughing again as I realized what kind of sexual tension I was going to endure for the next hour and set out to enjoy every second of the sweet torture. The initial breathing exercises sent new rushes of tingling to the surface of my skin and even through the thick cotton, my nipples were obviously hard.

Everything moves slowly in Bikram yoga. Slow, controlled moves into exacting positions and it wasn't long before Ahsan was moving around the room helping place people as they should be. I was torn between my desire to show him how far I had come in my lessons and my desire to feel his hands on my body. "All good things to those who wait" I murmured and thought "I am surely going to do something off sooner or later." The stretching felt good and as my muscles slowly loosened so did the languid feeling in my body intensify. The throbbing in my genitals was so insistent I felt focused by it and was startled when his hands gently encircled my thigh to move it just so. It sent currents through me and I wondered if he was affected at all or if he had just been glad to see an old friend. If he was paying attention as I knew he could, he had heard my soft gasp and knew I was affected by his touch. As he loosened his grasp he so very softly murmured "beautiful" and moved away. I was on fire and it was so delicious.

We all moved through the positions with slow graceful gestures and every time Ahsan approached my heartbeat would speed up and my skin tingle in anticipation. I didn't know how much more I could stand when he decided to push me further. I was lying down; we were almost done and in our final relaxation stretch when he knelt beside me and picked up my bottle of water. My body was heated at this point and when he poured the water over my chest I couldn't restrain the sharp intake of air. "He has to know what this is doing to me" I thought and as I looked up at him, he gently laid a single finger upon my lips and slowly winked, a smile playing in the corner of his mouth. "He is too effing gorgeous for my own good" I thought as my heart tripped over the implications. New waves of throbbing took over and I couldn't wait for everyone to leave.

I took my time in the dressing room letting the mass of the crowd clear and when I came out, he was waiting in the hall leaning against the wall with his arms crossed and a half grin on his face. "Oh yes" I thought, "he knows exactly what he has done to me" and I started to smile.

***

Shall I continue this some other time? I do believe I could write this story out further as I have enjoyed what I have done so far. I hope you have a lovely day D,
~Miselena

January 13

My Pet,

I can appreciate your exhaustion and the effort that you have put forth to please. Brutal oh no; demanding, uh maybe…

I think we both had only our appetites wet by our verbal exchange, and yes I did sense you were uncomfortable with the conversation regarding the oil, so I intentionally cut it short. Although, I will admit I was tempted to have you continue for the same reason. But we are not there yet. When we meet in person and we begin our physical sessions there will be plenty of time and opportunity for us to explore things that you once believed uncomfortable. As I said that only served to wet our appetite; I want more and I hope you do as well.

I am not surprised by your actions my dear but I do appreciate confirmation of what I see in writing from you. As you said it is much easier to put these things in writing. Although I wanted you to know that I am quite capable of vocalizing my desires and I was equally teased by your responses. We will have quite the time. I can tell from your responses you are as ready as I am to begin. Again I have to admit once we begin I will derive equal pleasure in watching you anticipate what is next and teasing you until you beg for the end. You will come to understand that during our sessions 'Yes Sir' is most appropriate and any other response (if a response is solicited at all) will be unwelcome.

As for your story, as always you are humble but incredibly good. I enjoyed it, and yes I want more. You are right; the scenario I presented you with has no winning outcome. You have left me wanting more; we will discuss payment for this in person. However, if you had provided nothing, your tab is getting rather extensive. You may wait until this weekend to complete your story and answer any lingering questions that have been left unanswered. I think that all things happen for a reason and perhaps my unexpected extension in Europe allows time for us both to get a bit settled. The beginning of the New Year is always hectic for me and it appears for you as well.

For now I will leave you with this thought; strength and sacrifice create humble success. You seem to have all these and I find no reason that our adventure together won't meet equal success capped with a bit of physical pleasure.
Good night my pet.

D

January 16

Hello D,

It is Friday night; about 9:00 and while I should be asleep, my body has suffered too much caffeine and Red Bull. My projects at work are coming along well and it looks like we have realistic completion dates on two of them. I am so thrilled; one project has been going for almost two years now. January is turning out to be a very good month. And I am moving into another apartment in February; same complex but one with a little more space and a view to die for. I am really excited about that, so things are good right now; busy but good. I hope your projects are going well over there.

You asked for two things in your last email; any lingering, unanswered questions (? I had to go back and look) and a continuation of my story. So you liked my story? That pleases me a great deal. I will do my best to do the first part justice but first... lingering questions... and here I thought I had answered them all... did I find humor? Humor – delight; it is really a matter of semantics. If we want to adhere to the strict definition of humor as defined by Merriam and Webster, then I suppose the answer is no. I equated being delighted with humor. And I often giggle when I am delighted with something.

Was I surprised? I am quite sure I answered that one. That leaves was I relaxed and able to drift into a real sense of pleasure. I suppose my answer to that was a bit ambiguous so to answer directly; not really. There were too many distractions going on... having to hold the phone, drifting in and out of focus... Don't get me wrong; it was lovely, but as I said, I think it will pale by comparison.

***

I took my time in the dressing room letting the mass of the crowd clear and when I came out, he was waiting in the hall, leaning against the wall with his arms crossed and a half grin on his face. "Oh yes" I thought, "he knows exactly what he has done to me" and I started to smile... No attempt on my part could keep it from turning into one of those silly, ear-splitting kinds of smiles, so I quickly ducked my head until I could get it under control as I approached him.

And then I saw his feet and looked up. He was so amused with me that in a flash, the smile was back. 'How can eyes so dark have so many lights'? I wondered. We stood there, the grand smiles slowly fading from our faces to be replaced with a look of intensity. It couldn't have been for long but it felt like we were reading each other's souls and the time just fell away. And then we were nodding, both at each other and Ahsan jerked his head toward the door. I followed him as he turned and headed into the rain, his never having said a word. I knew. He knew.

On the step he reached for my hand and gently pulled me into the rain. The rush of lunch-time traffic had disappeared and the sidewalk was surprisingly bereft of people. The air was heavy with humidity and as I raised my face to the rain, Ahsan stopped walking. I lowered my gaze and was immediately captured by his eyes; it felt like falling... In slow motion he pulled me into his arms and hesitated for the slightest moment, a mere breathe away from my lips. I couldn't help it I swear but a giggle of delight gurgled up out of my throat followed by a sharp gasp as the intensity slammed back into me. And then I saw it; that tiny dimple in the corner of his mouth that proved his pleasure. Once again he nodded his head and we were off.

Still we had not said a single word. It is a talent I think to be able to communicate clearly without speaking. One human's in general totally underestimate the value of. Imagine if you will if we were all deaf as a species. How fast I wonder, would telepathy develop? Very fast I would think. And so my mind wandered until I was pulled from my reveries and onto the walkway of an all too familiar residence. "Ahhh…" I thought. "I remember now…

I don't remember how it started…

I just remember doing…

What he told me..."

It was a relatively short walk from the cast iron gate to the massive oak doors but it felt interminable and surreal as if I was walking in slow motion. My mind flashed to the first night I had walked this path. It was dark then, not like now but the trepidation and excitement were the same none-the-less. No. That was a lie. The excitement was greater now. Much greater. I *knew* what was waiting for me beyond those doors. Before I only guessed.

The doors opened, as if by magic at the exact moment we arrived before them and once again I was reminded of the world Ahsan came from. A different world than those of us in the United States understood. A *very* different world; a world of total deference, total obedience.

We entered the receiving hall and Ahsan nodded at the footman as he closed the door and retreated down the hallway. We were alone. It was silent and the hallway was filled with candle light and the scent of incense. Ahsan pulled both my hands into his, commanding my gaze. I don't know how long we had stood there when he raised his gaze to the stairway and then lowered it to me.

Immediately I was on fire. Every inch of my skin tingled and I swear every hair stood on end. I couldn't breathe. Time stood still and flashbacks kept firing from my brain. Finally my body took over and I took a deep breath of air. "Damn"! I thought, as my head cleared. "I am gone," and I nodded, bowing my head.

The fact that I couldn't breathe properly didn't help as we climbed the stairway into the seemingly distant second level and I was truly breathless as we reached the landing and proceeded down a wing of the mansion into Ahsan's private suite of rooms. Candle light was everywhere; in the halls, in the rooms. It cast a soft golden halo on everything we passed. Music, at first faint but then stronger as we approached the suite began to make itself heard. It was soft, slow music… designed to relax and seduce. Ahsan wanted me pliable, and if I didn't know better, I would have said the setting was planned.

I was led beyond a final set of double doors, beautifully carved with intricate images of India. I couldn't breathe again. Everything in this room was deceptive. On the surface it looked harmless, exotic. Silk draped everywhere, cushions strewn seemingly haphazard. So opulent; so decadent, so very breath-taking. I knew better.

We no sooner approached the bed when Ahsan snapped one of the silk hangings framing the massive bed down and caressed the side of my face with the soft silk. Gently he brushed it down over my cheeks and lips, over my chin and down my throat. He moved behind me, slowly, fluidly. I was so attuned to his every move, every breath. Every move produced fresh waves of pleasure radiating through every pore of my body.

Both hands caressed my shoulders and I felt his breath against my neck, breathing in my scent. Slowly his hands drifted down my arms and he nuzzled my neck, gently biting at the nape. Every nerve was at attention… it was seconds away….

And then it came and a sense of release filled my body as my wrists were pulled behind my back and firmly secured by the silk in Ahsan's hand… there was no turning back now. The silk felt firm against my wrists and Ahsan made sure it would not slip loose. I felt myself sway into him and quickly corrected the movement.

'Keep your head girl' I thought while my body betrayed every rational thought I could throw at it. 'Let go… let go… le go…' And as soon as I did, the most luscious, languid sense of pleasure filled every stretch of my being.

Slowly he entwined my hair in his fist at the nape of my neck and pulled down… slowly, firmly, arching my back and neck and in doing so, making a perfect target of my neck. My breath was in pants by now, so excited I was…

***

It is now 1:30 am D and I must rest. I wish you a fabulous day,

~Miselena

January 18

Good Morning Miselena,

I trust it will be morning by the time you receive this. It was very nice reading your most recent email. Sounds like things at work are going quite well; it is so satisfying when a major project hits a significant milestone or better yet comes to completion. We are working several projects over here and they are all going quite nicely; it is interesting to see how world politics and world finances parallel each other. They are often married to each other.

The weather here today in Southern Italy is gloomy; it is drizzling and the temperature is a bit nippy. When I look into the distance the topography reminds me of the central California wine country. Mountainous and green it can be quite breathtaking but there is nothing like the US with its diversity, technology and freedoms. Traveling is an awesome experience and I have been most fortunate but we are extremely fortunate to live in America and I think when I return this time I will appreciate the 24hr 7/11 just a little bit more.

Your story was very nice, very, very nice! I must meet this Ahsan. Seriously I enjoy reading these thoughts from you. It truly gives me a sense of your persona and like me I think you enjoy the anticipation of the event as much as the execution of the event. This is not to say that the act itself is not satisfying in any way but the build up and then the performance, yes! You must have both for complete satisfaction.

By the way you mentioned that hearing Miselena for the first time was a bit different for you. I must say saying your name was a bit different for me as well, I enjoyed it, and I think I will enjoy calling you "My pet" as well we will see.

Your story flowed so well it captured the sense of eroticism while in public but unbeknownst to anyone other than the two primaries. It was great and I love these types of scenes. Imagine if you will a woman working out in the gym without panties, shorts that are loose yet can be manipulated to provide a peak of the treasure between her legs if she so desires. The woman works out with her husband or boyfriend and has noticed a gentleman that is quite attractive. Her boyfriend nods and she positions herself to provide inappropriate glimpses of the excitement between her legs to this stranger. She notices that he is equally attracted to her and follows her movements so that he is better positioned to enjoy his view. He never makes contact, never exchanges a word (a perfect gentleman) yet through the entire workout she is the object of his attention and desires. The woman continues in this manner for over an hour and at the conclusion of the workout her sex is drenched not from sweat but from the excitement of sex without intimacy. As she leaves the gentleman finishes up and sensing an opportunity the boyfriend follows them to the locker room (male and female rooms are adjacent with a shared hall) but stays far enough behind to allow something to happen. The stranger catches up to the beautiful woman and introduces himself and says, "That was quite a workout" the woman responds with one simple sentence. "Give me your finger", the stranger obliges and without drawing any attention she stands with her legs slightly open, lifts one leg of her shorts just high enough to allow his finger to run over the outer edges of her labia. She says "have a taste" as he puts his fingers to his mouth the boyfriend comes around the corner announcing "Baby are you ready yet" as if he is completely unaware of what she is doing, as if he has seen nothing, yet she knows he has seen it all. She smiles and says "honey this is (name)" He was explaining some new movements to me. The boyfriend says "thanks (name)", the boyfriend says "baby we gotta go" and she says "bye" to ...." and thanks"

Perhaps I would have you give me the show, but Miselena that would be too easy, too vanilla, anyone could do that. No me? I would place my collar on you, command you to change into something I have provided and then place a hood over your head and have you give me and whomever an anonymous show. That would suit us better. We would watch while you follow my instructions to the letter kneeling with your legs spread open masturbating to completion and then pleasing us until your hands are covered with the seminal fluid that tells you we have been thoroughly satisfied as well.

But perhaps that would be only the beginning. I would want to expose your well lubricated anal passage perhaps, displaying the treasures you have. How beautiful you are, how submissive you are and how proud I am that you are so eager to please. After the proper display and inspection you would hear me say you may smell "My pet" she smells so sweet and you will feel the breath of this stranger as he smells your skin feeling the heat of your body.

I know this excites you as I watch your breast movements, breathing deeper and deeper as your own excitement intensifies. You hear me say "My pet is incredible", and with that I grab your arms secure them behind your back, and raise you to your feet and bending you over to expose your open anus. I would provide the obligatory spanking because I love how your ass looks when it is just a bit pink...then slowly carefully work my rigid penis, so hard from the excitement of your spanking, into your anus... very, very slowly penetrating you from the rear. Next you hear my voice saying "yes you may taste it, it is incredible", and to your surprise you feel what appears to be a tongue on your swollen clitoris while I thrust deep into your ass.

I pull the back of the hood, which pulls your head back and whisper where your ears should be, "My dear you are incredible"

Enjoy your day Miselena,

D

January 19

Hello D,

I started this letter yesterday morning and got called away by work. It is now Monday night and will be your Tuesday morning. I have just poured a glass of wine and set

Enigma to playing and while your day has just started, mine is almost at an end. What would you have of me tonight I wonder? Your last email had not even one question. I was shocked and had to read it again to see if I had simply missed them but no, no questions, lol. I am teasing I hope you know because you usually ask a great many questions; are you running out I wonder or have you simply figured me out already, lol.

Now, that is not to say that your email has not raised some questions for me, for it has done that. Please, if you would, explain what a hood looks like to you? You have mentioned this apparel several times now and I would have a better understanding of what you are envisioning if it pleases you.

And we have graduated to active, third party participation in our fantasies; I do believe this is new territory.

So Italy looks something like but is nothing like home, eh? We are spoiled aren't we? I am truly thankful I was born here and not in some country like Saudi Arabia. With my demeanor? I would have been dead by 15. There must be benefits though, are you fluent in Italian yet? What other languages do you speak? That must be so cool. Languages were my minor in college and I have always loved them.

And you are enjoying my story; that pleases me more than I can say. However, if it appears that I enjoy the building anticipation as much as the act itself, it is only part of the story. The other part is an attempt to improve writing skills. I have been enjoying this a great deal and challenging myself to immerse the reader (you...) into the story by painting a better picture. The challenge to write better stuff is half the fun, and why it takes me so long to produce such small effort. But I cannot resist and will not be satisfied with anything less and nor, I imagine, would you.

I cannot wait until I am in my new apartment. There I wrote it; now maybe the thought will give me some peace...

Ah hell D, I am so excited about my new place I can't stand it. Damn. Patience is so easy on most subjects, then one pops up and bites you with its intensity. Time for another sip of wine.

Question from a previous email... my tab is raking up? Just how up is it, by the way?

I thought I might continue Ahsan's story. He is a Bikram yoga instructor. I don't remember his real name, I fabricated that too and I have only ever been to one of his classes. He is gorgeous and he did pour the water on my chest (and yes, I gasped) but that is the extent of any truth to that fantasy for it is that, a fantasy I have woven for your pleasure. Although I freely admit it has been for our pleasure for I have enjoyed it myself.

***

Slowly he entwined my hair in his fist at the nape of my neck and pulled down... slowly, firmly, arching my back and neck and in doing so, making a perfect target of my neck. My breath was in pants by now, so excited I was... he nuzzled my ear, breathing softly against the shell, reverberating, crashing against my pounding heartbeat, and then my head was raised back up. "Breathe"! I thought as I took a deep breath and he moved slowly in front of me, caressing my shoulder, over my collarbone, gently, so gently down the side of my breast.

I opened my eyes as he waited for me to do so and then a gentle smile formed on his lips. I knew what was coming and he was waiting to see if I would give up a response. I couldn't help forming a small smile of my own and that seemed all the answer he needed.

On the table was a sculpture of the Goddess Durga, the female warrior Goddess. It was, I suppose, a celebration of women to have this particular Goddess in Ahsan's quarters. She was incredibly detailed with many arms, one of which led a huge lion by a thick chain. I watched Ahsan touch the sculpture and as he caressed one of her arms he slowly pulled and a very sharp knife was revealed. I swayed and the candle light blurred in my vision as I took another deep breath.

The breathing didn't seem to help. I was in a fog and on fire and nothing I could do was going to ease that.

I had to wait for Ahsan to do that. And Ahsan liked taking his time.

He turned back to me, the smile having reached his eyes now and lowered his gaze to my clothes. "He is so beautiful" I thought, mesmerized. I watched as he grasped the bottom of my blouse and started to cut the lacings that held the front together. I never moved. I'm not even sure I breathed. Half way up he stopped and looked at me, searching… "What are you looking for" I wondered… as I felt myself falling deeper and deeper into his eyes. His gaze returned to his task and I took a deep breath watching the rest of my lacings go, one by one.

Slowly, one hand at a time he brushed back the silk of my blouse, his fingers spread; he gently caressed the crest of my breast avoiding the nipple. I wasn't wearing a bra. I could have been but those plans had changed in the dressing room. I had wanted this to happen, no doubt. My back was arched from the restraints on my wrists and my nipples were thrust out and clearly hard. I was breathing softly and watching his gaze as I saw it wander next to the straps over my shoulders. I no sooner thought "they're gone" when I heard the soft swish of silk as it swept to the floor leaving me naked from the waist up. He looked at me and smiled gently and started to speak for the first time.

"Why have you kept this beauty from me "? He asked and raised his eyes to mine.

As I opened my mouth to speak he laid a finger against my lips and murmured "Shhhh… I don't want to know… Are you mine now…? And be careful before you speak for I may decide to keep you Lisa". And I swam in the depths of his eyes. Once this was everything I wanted… once…

I gave the only answer I knew I could, and one I knew he would understand.

"I am yours today Ahsan…" I whispered, "And tomorrow will be as it is meant to be…"

He smiled; a slow, satisfied smile and I saw a new light come into his eyes and was immediately delighted and guarded by its implications.

My skirt went next, in one swift move and was pooled around my feet in a soft flutter. I was wearing nothing except my thong and high heels when I felt the blade of the knife slide against my skin and under the thin strap holding together the last piece of clothing I wore. He looked into my eyes – not at the thong - as he cut it off me, watching my reaction, measuring… and slowly an approving look emerged on his face and I knew I had pleased him.

He took me by the shoulders and turned me around and as he did so the room slowly came back into focus. Soft, muted light from the candles, silk hangings, opulent pillows and the silk from my wrists was loosened. He massaged my shoulders, reached down for my hand and pulled me forward saying "Come…"

***

I must quit for the night D, I hope your day is awesome,

~Miselena

Good Morning Miselena,

If I am lucky you will receive this in the morning and enjoy it with a fresh cup of hot coffee. I have intentionally provided you a breather (no tasking). You have been a bit overwhelmed at work and I want you to enjoy each experience without stress, therefore I have refrained from recent tasking. Your inquiry leads me to believe you enjoy my tasking as much as I and like me it is an enjoyable distraction from work and other things. Make no mistake I have not run out of wonder and until I am personally able to smell your soft skin, taste your sexual fluids, and caress your supple breast, I will remain intently frustrated and curious. 1st Question; you mentioned my story and the active engagement of another. What did you think of my story, did it create a swelling within you?

You asked what my expectation was with reference to a hood so I have attached a picture that is something like what I had in mind; however, I think the anticipation would be so much greater with the eyes covered.

Fluent in Italian? I think not but I do know enough to get what I need when I need it. I do enjoy listening to the language and the culture is so emotional even a simple hello can involve such expression as to appear argumentative, it is great! In my travels I have heard many languages; German, French, Italian, Czech, even the Queen's very own English.

Your tab, ah; I thought you would never ask. Your tab is now at a whopping 20. I have to ask Miselena would you take them all at once or would you beg to have your tab divided among sessions. I am sure you would be able to work it down a bit, if you were very, very obedient and accommodating. I guess it is good that you enjoy anal sex, oh and how good are your fellatio skills again?

So to answer your questions I have not lost interest in the least! My tasking will continue; see my next email. Oh by the way I would like a picture of your vagina displayed for me, specifically you standing with your legs open, and your labia spread wide preferably after a satisfying round of intercourse but if you are not sexually active right now I will accept the display only. Additionally I would enjoy a picture of a woman taking a man's penis in her ass; a picture that shows explicit penetration.

Yes, how I do enjoy your command of the written language. Your story is quite arousing. I must admit I was a bit surprised that you were so uncomfortable with the oral description of your oil experience, but even in that I drew some pleasure knowing that this description was not the norm for you. It will be so much easier for you to let go in person, mostly because it is easy for me to assume control; as long as your mind is willing, I will have your body!

For now I want you to think of how you will satisfy my request and take a moment to digest this picture.

Good night My Pet and yes tomorrow I will have real tasking for you!

January 20

Hello D,

I do enjoy your tasks, you are right; they are a lovely distraction from daily stresses and are indeed a source of discovery and pleasure. And I am pleased to hear you are intently frustrated and curious… two totally apt adjectives from this side of the ocean as well.

What did I think of your story? I loved your story. I enjoy the vast majority of them and this was no exception. The introduction of another man has long been a curiosity of mine and when you wrote of feeling his tongue on my clit as you penetrated my anus, I got very hot. Indeed, I am now as well and have the most delightful, heavy, throbbing feeling in my genitals. I do believe we could be setting a record for the longest foreplay session on Earth…

And 20? I think 20 is exceedingly good considering the length of time we have been at this. Hell D, you ought to dismiss them on those grounds alone… lol. I must have been a very good girl in the last three months to have only earned 20. Do I want them all in one session? I don't know… I cannot judge that yet and I will let you be the judge of my fellatio skills.

I have attached, for your pleasure, the two pictures you have requested; I hope they do indeed please you.

Have a lovely day D,

~Miselena

January 21

My pet,

How beautiful warm and inviting your vagina looks. Indeed we are setting the foreplay record but then I expect a wonderful release once we begin our physical pleasure. Oh back to your picture, your ass truly interests me. I can see the pucker of your anal passage peeking between your legs as you lift your vagina to give me full access.

A third participant is inevitable for us Miselena. I will afford you the time necessary for us, you and I to be completely comfortable and satisfied with each other but it is inevitable! In my mind you are bound and perfectly still. Your movements calculated because you know the repercussions of disobedience, although I kow you sometimes enjoy my repercussions.

Yes only 20 and we will begin slowly to test your endurance. How I long to share your tolerance for our play; to witness your endurance and commitment to please. You will be tested, and your tolerance for pain tested as well, and although I do not enjoy marking of any type, I do enjoy the warmth and rosy color that is the result of a well controlled spanking.

It is my intent to stretch your mind as well as your body and in doing so it will not be uncommon for you to please me, masturbate for our pleasure and to share your beauty while plenty of attention is given to your genitals and nipples. This attention is often best experienced with multiple individuals, you with your hood and each of us on a nipple while your hands are bound behind your back, teasing your body, rimming your anus while the other tastes the sweet juices that flow so freely between your legs. Imagine the sight of me spreading your cheeks wide open exposing you to our pleasure.

I can see even now your expression as you experience orgasm after orgasm from the oral stimulation that is yours. Yes my pet you will cum and it will please us both (you and I).

It is now time for your mission/task; first I want you to go to the market or grocery store and purchase a cucumber. I want you to make sure you clean the cucumber thoroughly, get the olive oil you used before. I want you to close your eyes drift into your mind, imagining the scene of my previous email, allow the oil to drip over your clitoris and massage it gently into your labia, running your fingers over your lips and engorged clit.

Do this very, very gently; the oil should feel exquisite against your soft shaved skin, imagine this as my tongue running over your wet sex, penetrating occasionally to drink from the well that is our pleasure. Take the cucumber and slip it inside of your inviting vagina, does it fill you completely? Now take the clothes pin and clamp them to your nipples; apply 2-3 to each breast then run the tips over your nipples several times, do this to each breast, over and over. Do not forget to remove the clothes pins frequently.

Have I ceased wondering? Not even close my pet....

The picture you sent has brought me pleasure, here is a show of my satisfaction.

Where will you be this weekend, I think I would enjoy a chat Saturday evening if you do not have other plans.

January 21

Hello D,

I hope you have had an awesome day and you were pleased with my pictures. And your picture; that was for me, really? Specifically me, I mean; I gave you *that* specific hard-on? That's a nice thought. We have to work on the resolution of your photos though D although I have to say you have an exquisite body, have I told you that before? You really do; you are going to be such a pleasure to touch. Mmmm… and you write such intoxicating passages. I fall into them so totally and can feel what you suggest on my body. I get so hot D. Should I bite my tongue and *not* say I am growing impatient? But then I have waited 46 years for this experience so I suppose I can wait a bit more.

I have purchased the cucumbers and they are warming to room temperature as we speak. Ice cold I'm afraid will not do so I will report on that tomorrow. Shall I tease you a bit and tell you that I bought *two*? I'm not so keen on the marker idea but I will, as you know, comply and tell you how I felt about it.

Have a lovely day,

~Miselena

January 22

Yes Miselena, I truly enjoyed your picture; I enjoyed it so much I had to clean myself after my enjoyment. Oh and thank you for the compliment on my body. It is good to see we are mutually attracted. I am equally attracted to your body and I can not wait to fill each of your areas of pleasure with my tongue, my penis and...

Also, I appreciate your gracious compliments on my writing. I have a long way to go. All too often my thoughts get ahead of my fingers; as you well know it is difficult to ensure you do not skip details that will fill the scene and make the fantasy complete, thank you.

As for the gift you present me (you), I will take care to appreciate all your treasures and although I will command you during our sessions, the pleasure will be ours. You will detect my respect for the gift you give and even in that you will be encouraged to give me all. The times we share in our fantasies will soon be brought to reality!

Oh yes Miselena it would be a tease for you to tell me you have two cucumbers as we will have no instant gratification when we are together, it will be prolonged ecstasy and I will derive pleasure from the control you will eagerly give to me.

My pet I am very, very anxious to hear the results of your most recent tasking, including your thoughts on the markers. Tell me Miselena have I truly surprised you with any of my tasking so far?

Have a beautiful day, and take care of that beautiful body until such time as I can feel your skin as the palm of my hand strikes your firm ass.

D

January 22

Hello D,

I had a lovely day thank you, and I hope yours will be quite lovely and productive as well. I have to admit, when you write the word 'soon', I wonder what that means... so totally subjective, isn't it? And once again you have (either knowingly or not), paid me a beautiful compliment with your comments on respect. I truly believe respect is one of those qualities you have to earn so for you to say the things you have means a great deal to me and speaks highly of the trust and faith we have built together so far. What think you on this subject?

And so I succeeded in teasing you a bit with the cucumbers, eh? Well I did buy two as it so happens and I will admit that I took the time to measure the circumference as I selected them. If anyone had been truly watching me they would have known my purpose right away. I actually laughed as I did it in the store. I have become shameless D, and it's all your fault.

Needless to say they were chosen for their aptitude toward the application and I did choose to employ them both. I have been craving some anal sex you understand, and not having had the opportunity to enjoy that in a while, I decided to take it upon myself. Damn D, I am so hot right now... I wish you were here...

Here's the deal; it was lovely and I had a nice orgasm but, and this is a pretty big but, it was just ok because it was just *me*. Do you understand? I got off because I needed to get off but it was not the kind of explosive, heart pounding orgasm that you experience with another person. That I suppose, is what I am really craving right now. The markers didn't do anything for me at all. I don't know if it was because the feeling was so light after the intensity of the clothes pins or what, but there it is. I hope I haven't disappointed you but the truth should not for it is what it is and I have decided to be totally honest in this.

I am going to be working this weekend again, but I promise to find some time to write more of Ahsan's story; that is a promise to me as much as it is a promise to you. I have come to enjoy writing D, and that is all your fault too. Thank you for that, thank you very much.

~Miselena

January 23

Oh my dear you are quite shameless. First let me say you are absolutely correct, soon is subjective and with this I do not attempt to tease or prolong this agony for either of us. In this I will be absolutely honest; I have not given a specific date because when I do, I want to ensure there are no obstacles that will hinder our meeting.

Oh now back to shameless... it is not shameless that you are my pet, but open and adventurous and this is an asset that will serve you well my dear. There will be a time when you will perform this same act, only in the distance I will be watching perhaps even talking to you on the cell phone while you pick and choose a vegetable of my choosing.

So you see my dear, this task, as many of my tasks do, has a separate agenda; we will do this again, with me in the background watching and perhaps not even you will know where I am watching from. You will be directed not to seek out my location but to only obey my direction. To look for me when we do these types of events will only serve to increase the number 20 I have been so conservative with.

Do I understand - why yes my dear I certainly do, like you I too have female friends and even a steady female friend in the states but, the intensity of the orgasm I have with vanilla partners pale in comparison to my true desires. Our dilemma is that only someone that has an affinity for the "lifestyle" can appreciate and even participate in the sensual acts we have described.

Respect for you, you have no idea because it is the courage that we have that allows us to do things that others secretly dream of, fantasize about and masturbate to. We have the courage to go beyond what someone else might classify as normal (keep in mind I am not talking dark, dark extremes). I absolutely abhor prudish women, and men but that is not to say I do not appreciate 'class'. There is a distinct difference between 'letting go of your inhibitions' and being vulgar and disgusting. We will 'let go' and in that we will experience the most powerful orgasms together!

Now I will have to tell you that you have been remiss; you have not provided me the level of detail I desire with reference to the actual act! I want to know when you came were you filled in your vagina and anus? I want to know do you cum with the clothes pins attached or removed? Did you dream, envision me spanking your ass while you came or were you thinking of me and my friend having you vaginally, and anally? Consider this my pet; I am equally hot and want to play, scene, display you in so many ways and as my desire grows my patience grows inversely Short answer; I want you to serve me in the worst way. I want you to submit yourself completely to me, I want you to perform, display and satisfy our desires, I want to see your face, your expressions when you experience your first orgasm with me. I want to see your face and hear your voice when you receive your first spanking. I want to watch your expressions, body language when I bind you, and have you kneel to please my black shaft for the first time!

You crave anal sex my dear and I crave your obedience we shall both be completely satisfied.

Now provide me the details I have requested.

With regards to anal sex, as I have always said I love it and you will be amply taken care of in that area, over and over and over...

Would you like to chat for a bit Saturday night or are you otherwise engaged for the evening?

Oh thank you for all your compliments; I will continue to cause you to do things that will be both a mental a physical test, even after I return. The difference will be that after I return we will set up the physical demonstrations of your tasking.

As always I enjoy reading your writing as much as you enjoy the writing and I will anxiously await your continuing story about Ahsan.

Thank you so very much and we will discuss the marker experience at a later time, have a good evening my dear.

D

January 23

Hello D,

I hope you are having an awesome morning; it is Friday night and I am going to try to get to sleep early as I need to rest. I will be working tomorrow day but I am all yours tomorrow night. Just let me know what time to be online and there I will be.

So I didn't give you enough detail? Hm... I suppose I can provide that. When I actually came I only had one inserted and that was anally. The other was too large to allow the simultaneous accommodation of the second and so they were used one at a time. I do believe the clothes pins were attached at the time and I remember laughing at your admonishment to not keep them on for too long as I was removing them, having lost track of any sense of timing. And I was visualizing anal sex at the time though if I remember aright, there may have been a spank or two involved... I'm not sure anymore... that was two days ago and the details have begun to fade. I do however, have the recollection that I was disappointed and that that kind of fun was better shared than done alone.

More tomorrow...

~Miselena

January 24

Hello D,

I am looking forward to our chat tonight and in the meantime I thought I might continue with a bit more of Ahsan's story...

***

He took me by the shoulders and turned me around and as he did so the room slowly came back into focus. Soft, muted light from the candles, silk hangings, opulent pillows and the silk from my wrists was loosened. He massaged my shoulders, reached down for my hand and pulled me forward saying "Come…"

We crossed the room, his steps silent against the floor while mine echoed behind him, my eyes following the pattern of inlaid stone. It was such exquisite craftsmanship and I reflected once again on the unassuming opulence of Ahsan's world. We paused before a curtain of gossamer silk so sheer the multitude of candles gleaming beyond cast softly muted halos upon it and they glistened as we swept the silk aside. Ahsan waited, standing perfectly still as he allowed me to see what had been so carefully planned beyond. 'How…' I thought, stunned for a moment; 'how did he pull this off'? And then I knew. He had planned for this before I had ever left the dressing room. Confusion swept over me, as fully a rush as the warmth that flushed my skin and I was awed and touched by his thoughtfulness. This was going to be fun; it was going to last for hours and it was going to be exquisite. 'Oh you really want to spoil me' I thought as I looked at him in wonder.

He smiled with that indefinable sense of masculine assurance and satisfaction that is so intoxicating and then slowly his eyes grew intense and searching. "It would always be like this…" he whispered, locking his eyes with mine, his voice vibrating with passion.

I couldn't breathe. I felt as if my body had been plunged into the ocean as a wave of cold then hot rushed from the tip of my skull to the tips of my toes and back. Every hair on my body felt electrified and if he had merely brushed my clit with his hand at that moment I would have exploded. My body's need for oxygen took over and as it gasped a deep breath of air my head began to clear. I thought to myself 'one day at a time' and resisted the overwhelming urge to say "Ah, Okay!" as a smile formed in the corner of my mouth at the thought.

Ahsan stepped closer, cupped the back of my head with his hand and with is other hand still holding my own, placed it in the small of my back and pulled me forward. Ahsan is tall but I have long legs and with the additional height of my heels this placed my genitals softly and firmly against his own. I was aching by now and I wouldn't have believed my heart could have pounded any harder when he started to lower his mouth to mine. A sigh of bliss slipped through my lips as he ever so gently brushed his lips against mine, breathing in my scent as he did. And then there was that smile back, the one that lingered in the corner of his mouth betraying his amusement at my torment and obvious absorption. He started to pull away and had no sooner moved six inches when a soft black sheath of silk descended over my eyes and was securely fastened behind my head. Only then did I recall what had been waiting for me in that room as it quickly flashed in my mind.

Candles had been everywhere casting the room in a soft, undulating gold, sensuous in its movement. Incense had been burning in a large brass pot on the floor filling the air with the sweet, heady scent of sandalwood. I knew when the time came it would be used to scent my body and the throbbing in my genitals grew more intense. Several pair of hands gently caressed my arms slowly moving down to my hands and started to pull me forward. 'How many attendants were there…'? I thought as I began to move; I couldn't remember but thought there were at least three. And these were attendants, I knew from their dress which was traditional Indian costume in all its rich color, bare foot with elaborate ankle bracelets decrying their station in life.

They drew me to a stop and I felt the presence of a man behind me. He wrapped his arm around my waist and bade me to lean against him. I don't think it was Ahsan. I felt a pair of hands slowly glide down my legs, starting at the thigh and while one stopped just behind the knee, the other continued down to my ankle and grasped it firmly, lifting it from the floor. My heels were removed, first one then the other and I was bent over forward from the waist, my hands placed on either side of what I remembered being a wide, thickly padded bench in the room. "There is one step in front of you" said one of the attendants, "step up and stretch out. Put your arms up over your head." And I complied, eager to begin.

In India preparation for sex could be almost as much fun as the act itself, especially if one has attendants trained in arousal and Ahsan certainly did. It was decadence of the most extraordinary kind. I felt my hair being brushed as oil was worked into my body at several points beginning at my fingers and toes. My arms quickly graduated to my shoulders and as I was groaning from the pleasure I felt strong hands massage and kneed my buttocks. 'Ah…' I thought and let go letting a warm, languid feeling suffuse my behind, tingling in anticipation.

Slowly a warm hand slid over the curve of my buttocks and slipped into the folds of my labia, penetrating for only a second and then out and back up my cheek gently pulling it aside. Then two hands on either side, slowly moving down. The oil on my body felt so smooth and I gasped at the pleasure I had as two fingers were inserted and the second hand ever so lightly brushed against my clit. Back again and the hands sweep back and firmly pulled my cheeks apart, exposing my anus. I feel warmed oil dripping on me and yet another hand came into play. I groaned as the first finger slid in my rear, twirling it slightly from one side to the other; I gasped as the second finger slid in, twirling slowly, firmly widening the passage, preparing me for my session with Ahsan and knowing all the while he was there, watching, touching along with all the other hands.

"Enough!" I heard him say, in what sounded to my delighted ears like impatience. "Dress her now" and I was drawn up and soon standing. The blindfold was removed and I smiled as I faced a wall of mirrors and could see every preparation. My hair was brushed back and pinned with an exquisite silver chain, intricately wrought draping to a heart shaped pendant that lay against my forehead with a single, silver tear hanging from the point. Elaborate silver earrings were placed on my ears and as my hands and body were draped in silver, kohl was applied to my eyes and henna to my fingers and toes. I was still naked, but dressed in silver, the most provocative being a slender silver strand spanning my waist spaced with tiny dangling hearts. The pot of incense was brought over and I was bade to spread my legs. The pot was placed between my legs and the smoke slowly rose up, curling around my thighs, drifting over my mound, dissipating as it reached my hips, scenting my body with the musky, sweet scent of sandalwood.

My eyes drifted closed as I let the incense drift over my body. I felt so relaxed, so at ease with the world, so languid. It was a gift Ahsan was giving me tonight, no doubt. How extremely wonderful and how blessedly welcome. No need to think, no need to control, manipulate, maneuver. Just feel and enjoy. I opened my eyes, ready and anxious to go to Ahsan. I knew he waited for me. I felt pampered and beautiful and wanted to bow at his feet in supplication.

Ah D, that is all for now, talk with you soon,

~Miselena

February 9

Miselena,

My apologies my dear I was called away on an emergency in Malta and have been completely unattached from my electronic communications. I returned yesterday and I am still digging myself out from under my email. In fact, if you sent me an email during this period it was most likely rejected because my account was overflowing. Have you continued your Ahsan epic and how is the new apartment? Yes I know I should be back in the states now, but this trip to Malta has set me back once again.
Write soon, and we will discuss.

D

February 9

Ah D,

It is so good to hear from you. I have been busy myself (talk about an understatement) and am T - 8 days and counting to the systems conversion I have been working on. I have *not* written any more and have missed the exercise but I am hoping to correct that after this conversion is done. THEN, I am going to take a vacation... long over due and well deserved and get my life back to some semblance of normalcy.

I am in my new apartment and absolutely love it. I have attached a few pictures of the view from my balcony and every morning I am elated to wake up to this view; it is an awesome way to start my day - not to mention close it out.

So you have been in Malta... I hope that there was at least some small part of that trip that was pleasurable. It has been beautiful here and you couldn't ask for a more pleasant winter; truly we are all being spoiled rotten.

Let me know when you catch up... its good to hear from you.

~Miselena

February 9

My goodness what a spectacular view, the sail boats and water make that such a tranquil setting how could you do anything but appreciate your blessings, wow!
Believe it or not Malta was nice but oh boy, incredibly expensive. I'm not a big fast food fiend but I had to eat and run a few times, how does a whopper, fries and coke for $9.00 grab you. But that being said it is rich in history and has seen/participated in a great many battles for such a small island. I have to be honest I was quite ignorant of many things prior to my first visit to the island.

As for you my pet when are you going on vacation and when will you return? Going anywhere special? Will there be a great deal of sex involved or just peaceful indulgence, which is sometimes just as satisfying depending on your partner.

Word of encouragement, do not give up on our adventure as the famous Clint Eastwood once said, "Endeavor to persevere". Our desires and interest are too close for me to let an opportunity such as this slip away, I will "endeavor to persevere" smile.

D,

February 9

By the way do not think that I have forgotten that you owed me a chapter of Ahsan, and now you owe me much more (10).
Grand Total 30, some things are just priceless.

February 10

Hello D,

I hope you had an awesome day, or rather that you will too. I have to admit, I grow more curious about what you do and are doing; dashing off to Malta for ten days and Malta even has a McDonald's? That seems almost blasphemous. So how is the Mediterranean this time of year? Is it beautiful? I will be going to Florida first, to Clearwater on the Gulf Coast. The sand there is like fine white, crystalline powder and the waters are every shade of blue-green to deep blue you can imagine. It will be far enough into spring that the weather should be perfect. I am visiting my sisters on this trip, the last week or so of March and one is coming from Texas. So no, there will be absolutely no sex this week but I haven't seen my sisters in too long so who cares? This vacation is sure to be lively for my family is a feisty bunch and often I find myself in the position of peacemaker. Then I am going to work one week and take a second vacation.

This one I'm not as sure of... as to exactly what I plan to do. It will be somewhere warm and with any luck, with someone. We will see.

And now I owe you more of Ahsan and I am being penalized for not having written already; I say again my friend; you are brutal. But I won't go on, I will endeavor to persevere....

Your segment tonight may be short for I am pressed to the wall right now and time is my most precious commodity. And it takes me time to compose a story; I am very self critical on this point and it has to live up to or surpass what I have already done. I have not forgotten your challenge but I have to warn you it will happen when the story dictates the timing is right. Right now I think Lisa has a few more adventures in store before the actual possession of her occurs...

***

My eyes drifted closed as I let the incense drift over my body. I felt so relaxed, so at ease with the world, so languid. It was a gift Ahsan was giving me tonight, no doubt. How extremely wonderful and how blessedly welcome. No need to think, no need to control, manipulate, maneuver. Just feel and enjoy. I opened my eyes, ready and anxious to go to Ahsan. I knew he waited for me. I felt pampered and beautiful and wanted to bow at his feet in supplication.

Once I had been new to Ahsan's world. I hadn't known what kind of delights were in store. I had been incredibly naïve and incredibly curious. I don't know if the anticipation then or now was greater; I couldn't think beyond the throbbing in my body and the pounding of my heart as I stared at myself in the mirror, mesmerized in a moment of intense stillness.

I awoke from my trance in the next moment as if startled and turned toward the silk curtain concealing Ahsan's bedroom. Without a word the attendants silently left the room, as if melting into the background leaving me alone. I started moving toward the curtain and sweeping it aside, paused on the threshold wanting to drink in and memorize every tiny detail. The candle light was soft and golden and shimmered off the silks that hung around the bed and in the pillows on the floor, moving and throbbing as if the light itself were alive.

The air itself was filled with the scent of incense and sweet almond candles. The music was soft, slow and seductive filled with deep rhythms that echoed in your soul. I was enchanted.

Well that was shorter than even I had hoped but I must sleep now... night

~Miselena

February 11

Hello D

I am in one of those moods where my mind is rambling so who knows what is going to come of tonight's correspondence. I just can't seem to settle on one subject too long before I am off to another; work mostly as I have so much to do and I am struggling not to feel overwhelmed. I feel like I am about to be graded – and in reality I probably am – and am beginning to feel that numbness and sense of the surreal that happens when you know events are unfolding before your eyes and now that the ball has gained enough momentum, it is no longer within your ability to control. Too many people are involved now for that and this project has taken on a life of its own. If you are a praying man, say a prayer for me; I am T – 6 days and counting.
I really must stop this. No more work tonight. I owe us both more of Ahsan.

***

The music soft, slow and seductive was filled with deep rhythms that echoed in your soul. I was enchanted. I was humbled.

I searched the room for Ahsan and not seeing him, frowned in curious anticipation, every nerve immediately on the alert. These rooms were deceiving and well I knew it to be true in fact. The silk hangings on the walls hid secret passages; the mirrors were transparent from behind. You never knew who was watching or who could enter, and in Ahsan's home, everyone moves silently. Suddenly I felt a rush of adrenaline, like a cold wave wash over my body and every inch of my skin from my fingertips to my toes began to tingle. 'What as he done'? I thought, 'And how much could he have planned in such a short period of time? I didn't spend that much time in the dressing room...'

My heart was pounding as I moved into the room, muffling the sound of the music. My face felt flushed. I paused only a moment as a wry smile emerged on my face that quickly turned into a grin. I had been here before. I knew exactly what to do. Relax, release and let go. Submit to Ahsan in whatever he chose. Ahsan could be a most generous lover when he was pleased and a most forbidding master when he was not. He had expended a great deal of effort to please me today and I would expend a great deal more to him in passion.

I crossed the room and out to the balcony and looking out, simply waited. I knew it wouldn't be long before I was approached and I smiled as I gazed down over an intimate private courtyard. There was a gracefully arched staircase leading down from the end of the balcony and the setting was peaceful beyond words. An exquisitely carved marble fountain nestled in the hibiscus and oleander. Jasmine climbed the walls and filled the air with its sweet scent. Azaleas blanketed the base of the dogwood tree that stood in the corner and provided a lacy canopy of white blossoms. Tiny lanterns peaked in and out of the shrubbery and… that fast my vision was taken away as I felt the silk scarf that had been placed over my eyes firmly secured in place. I had not heard a sound and found that while I was startled, I was not surprised.

"Lisa", Ahsan whispered, "I don't know if I should be pleased that you are here or displeased that you have kept yourself from me for so long". I knew better than to talk and simply bowed my head, totally still and submissive. I knew he would never take me in anger and so wanted him to be pleased in an almost desperate way. We stood for several moments as I waited for Ahsan to asses his feelings and decide. It seemed like a very long time when I felt the need to make a gesture to him; something that would assuage his pain and please his soul. Slowly I turned around toward him and knelt, sitting back on my heels and with my elbows extended, placed my hands in prayer and worship position. I swear I could feel the tension ebb from his body and it wasn't long before I knew he was smiling.

I could feel Ahsan; though we weren't touching, I could feel his presence and the sudden heat of desire that rolled off his body and I knew he was hard. I wanted him in my mouth and I wanted it now. I wanted to please him and caress his phallus with my hands and lips, firmly grasping the root and teasing the head with soft fluttery licks slowly encircling the crown and drawing it into my mouth. 'Oils would be nice right now' I thought as I immersed myself deeper and deeper into the fantasy, cupping his testicles and gently massaging them.

"Come Lisa" I heard as it slowly penetrated my consciousness and I gathered myself with a deep breath and stood.

***

Anticipation is a good thing don't you think? And I don't want this story to end too quickly; I am enjoying it all too much to rush through without properly putting all the pieces in place. There is much more to this story I already know and maybe we will both be surprised where it eventually leads us.
I hope you have an awesome day D,

~Miselena

February 12

My goodness Miselena,
 Sounds like your schedule for the next couple of months will be quite full. As for seeing your sisters, sometimes time well spent with loved ones (family) can be just as good as sex. Ok well maybe not just as good but definitely enjoyable.

Now for Ahsan, let me say the story the other day was a very good teaser but I hungered for a glimpse into the depth of your passion. Today I was quite satisfied; it was pleasing to read your thoughts in this manner. It definitely brought a smile to my face and a pace to my heart that I have missed for the past few days. In your story today you have given me many hints and I will digest them, careful not to indulge in gluttony but to slowly savor each piece of this wonderful puzzle.

I will tell you that I am particularly enticed by your description of the oral pleasure Lisa has tempted Ahsan with. I can only imagine the skill at which you will satisfy our pleasure when we share our oral passion. Much like Ahsan I can be a very, very giving passionate lover and I particularly love the texture and feel of the female sex in my mouth. It is incredible even in thought to imagine your legs spread open before me while my mouth hovers over your passionate sex, taking you into my mouth in a long, slow deep kiss. Penetrating you with my tongue then slowly teasing the tip of your clitoris as I flicker my tongue gently over your hood, then taking your entire sex into my mouth alternating between gentle feather like teases and hot passionate penetration.

Yes if there is something I love more than anal sex it is oral sex but I will indulge myself in them all with you as my submissive partner and me as the powerful master. The pleasure will be mutual, the respect will be complete but the control will be mine!

February 12

Hello D,

My schedule is always full; time is my most precious commodity without a doubt. And you are absolutely right about the need to get on to the next project. It is like a drug and I find I want something new and challenging to work on; something I can get excited about. My next big project to finish off is re-designing our website. What is up right now is what we inherited when our team arrived onsite. On March 1 (or thereabout) we will go live with the changes (another one of my babies). Be sure to look at the old version because the new one will blow you away; it is so totally cool.

So you are enjoying Ahsan and beginning to wonder at my skills; that makes me smile. You alone can assess my skills however you have the advantage of many, many hints presented to you through the volumes of email we have exchanged. Are you getting anxious to meet me yet? I am anxious to meet you...

Have an awesome day D,

~Miselena

February 16

Hello D,

It is T – 1 day and we are not going to make our live date. Unless we get a miracle from God and you know; I bet He's busy with more important things. And I have to say it is as much my company's fault as it is the software company's. Ugh... I sat down to write to forget about work for a while; I am just so frustrated now I want to scream and there is a knot in my stomach that is beginning to really ache. I need to relax so badly; I wish I knew some meditation techniques right now. Ahh... this just isn't working... I keep drifting back to work. I am poor company tonight and will write in a few days.

~Miselena

February 18

Miselena,

Do not be discouraged by the passing of your deadline; rather be encouraged that the product you will provide will ultimately satisfy all your customers needs. There used to be a saying when I first started doing what I do, 'if you want it bad, you'll get it bad' sometimes these things take time and although like me I detect your drive to perform is completely self-inflicted and only equaled by your drive to succeed. It pains you to when the expectation of performance is not met. Keep in mind, no one died today because of the passing of this deadline, now don't misunderstand just cause no one died does not mean you don't want to kill someone nor does it belittle the importance of what you are doing, not at all! Step back take a breather and knock there fucking socks off with the product you provide them and then watch them say 'Wow this was worth waiting for!'

Don't worry about the company, and I most definitely have some relaxation techniques that we will use; it is called obedience, my pet and it will be great!

***

I am beyond anxious right now. I am at the point of eruption. I cannot wait to direct your lips to my penis. To instruct you with my firm tone as you take me into your mouth tasting my pre-cum as it drips from the tip of my penis; my voice instructing you on exactly what I want and expect from you. In return I will clearly define what you will get from me as you watch my member grow from a flaccid penis to a stiff engorged and throbbing phallus.

Once you have me properly pleased and well lubricated, your anal cavity is the first stop on our little adventure but not before I employ some of my relaxation techniques. They include a bit of massage therapy and some other eccentric nuances. My technique involves slapping your ass vigorously then gently caressing the sting away only stopping to taste the sweet moisture I've created between your legs. Yes I would pause to taste and perhaps linger just a bit knowing that we both enjoy this oral temptation so intently.

Miselena my pet you do know how I love to tease so before we proceed I reveal that you are remiss in your shaving, it is not to my satisfaction and tonight I will show you what satisfies me, it is a special treat that you will enjoy but it does not come without a price. The cost; you must be bound and blindfolded. Immediately you assume a position that grants me complete access to your anus and genitals, lying down on your back with your knees folded your legs spread wide, as if I were to provide you a pelvic exam. I am already prepared and after you have been properly secured and blindfolded we begin.

The first sensation you feel is a hot, hot rag covering your entire sex, it is almost unbearable but in an odd way so stimulating. I remove the rag just to watch as your labia and clitoris swell with color, engorged with blood. I take your sex into my mouth and the sensation immediately propels you into a sense of euphoria. Again, the hot rag followed by more of my oral stimulation, finally you hear that you are almost ready so we must continue.

I have prepared some soothing, warm oil that I allow to drip over your pubic mound. It flows slowly, slowly down your swollen labia, and finally between your cheeks where it just teases your anus. I use my strong hands to massage the oil into your skin and again you feel an orgasmic sensation coming on, however, I stop this motion just short of your completion. Finally, you feel the razor gently gliding over your genitals, you can tell I am taking such care, which only serves to amplify the sensations you are feeling. You are completely wrapped up in the moment and your mind is filled with nothing but the here and now, the sensations you are feeling under my powerful presence. No work, no control, no thought just feelings, and it is awesome. Soon, too soon I am finished. Your desire to climax is overwhelming, but not quite yet my pet!

My attention quickly moves to your anus. Tonight I choose for you to have an anal orgasm, where I can feel each riveting spasm as you milk my penis with each powerful wave of your own climax.

Do you really need to ask about how anxious I am for us to get together?
D

February 18

Hello D,

Thank you for the words of encouragement; I am feeling much better today than I was the other night. The delay we are experiencing is (hopefully) only a one week set-back and we will know for certain by Sunday evening.

And thank you for your story too; it has been too many days since I have had a chance to read something not work related, never mind the time to write anything more. And I am missing writing almost as much as reading your letters.

I am in the midst of work right now and have to get back to it but I think I will have at least one day off this weekend. It is going to be a day of relaxation - regardless of the fact that I haven't done laundry in a month, I am going to do nothing that requires any expenditure of mental or physical energy. Except maybe write for I am missing that.

I hope your day is awesome; thanks again...

~Miselena

February 19

You are welcome,

In many ways sweet Miselena we are so much alike! We drive ourselves so hard that no one could be a better critic of us than we are of ourselves. I will write you a letter for your digestion this weekend. Something to take your mind off work, however brief that may be. Yes you do owe me a story but I owe you one as well so for now we are almost even. Oh I think you asked me once what I do, I thought I mentioned it before but if not I am in charge of major communication system installations for government facilities

114

abroad (sort of a troubleshooter). So if you ever wonder if I truly understand the stress and impact of deadlines, contracts, and budgets, let me put your mind at ease, I am intimately familiar with all of the above.

D

February 19

Hello D,

I hope you are having an awesome day. My day today was more relaxing and I am gathering my resources for the final push. Funny isn't it, how that phrase applies to both the business environment and labor, as if you are truly giving birth to something new? You have been wonderfully supportive and encouraging throughout my entire diatribe and my gratitude on this knows no bounds. Thank you very much.

I am my own worst critic and I have not yet determined if it is a good or bad thing. I suppose it is mostly good; what do you think? I am looking forward to your letter by the way, I love your stories. I will get back to Ahsan just as soon as this madness fades to a dull roar.

I must rest now D; be safe.

~Miselena

February 23

First my pet let me say, there is only one true way to show your limitless gratitude. Should I make you guess? No I think not; I will tell you directly your gratitude will be acknowledged through your servitude to our pleasure.

I think my pet now is a good time to chat, I will be on Wednesday night about 8:00 pm if you are available we can share some more secrets and surprises.

***

Today, I call you and tell you to prepare yourself for me tonight. My list is extensive with details down to the perfume you are to wear. You follow each instruction to the letter. Shortly after my call a box is delivered to your apt. It is wrapped in plain paper, and the name on it simply says Miselena followed by your address. This brings an instant warmth to your genitalia which surprises you a bit. On the package there is no return address, no distinct markings at all but from the address you know it is from me and you know that you must open it in the privacy of your apt.

Inside is a brief note that reads 'The leather is for you, put it on!' Inside you find leather heels, a corset, leather gloves, a micro-mini leather skirt, and underneath it all a huge, soft rubber phallus. Some time later you hear a knock and you know instinctively it is me. You open the door and drop your head automatically, humbly submitting yourself to me without a word. You know this is how I like it. I enter and you are wearing the gift I've sent. It fits perfectly and you appear distinctly feminine yet incredibly erotic.

I lean to you and whisper softly in your ear, "remove my clothes" and you respond obediently taking off first my jacket and shirt, slowly allowing yourself to feel my skin and the muscular frame of my body. The anticipation this creates is unbearable for both of us and as you remove my pants you see that you have created a bit of excitement in me, you smile but do not lift your head.

Excellent, my pet I must be pleased before we play. That is your cue to take me into your mouth and engulf the swollen crown of my penis, yes my dear nice, very nice. Now where is my gift? You are all too aware of the gift I am mentioning and on the table it lay. The huge phallus, foreboding and ominous yet your curiosity has you dripping with excitement.

How will we use this? Could you take it all? You hear me say, this is a test of your servitude my pet, turn around and bend over, and for the first time I detect a bit of apprehension, but slowly you comply hoping that I truly do not attempt to fill your anus with this monstrosity.

Should I continue with my surprise....?

D

February 23

Good Morning D,

I hope you are having an awesome day. We are going to attempt to go live once again this week and I am hoping we can actually pull this off. I have my doubts but I am reserving final judgment until Tuesday evening.

You have guessed very well D, but not close enough. I will say you are half right on one of your guesses and that is more of a hint than I would have given my sisters.

I will do my best to be online at 8:00pm Wednesday but my schedule this week is at the mercy of this project so I cannot promise. Most likely I will be there as it would take a great deal to keep me away.... I so enjoy our chats.

How goes your project by the way? Any eta yet? Methinks a little bit of D in the flesh would go a long way toward alleviating some of my stress...

Be safe,

~Miselena

February 24

Good Morning Miselena,

Well let us both hope that your go live date is a go and you are right, A little D would go a long way to soothe the stress beast.

Now Miselena, I do love a bit of intrigue. Getting close am I. Well here comes the tough part which half have I gotten right? I will do my best not to let my curiosity get the best of me but I will readily admit you have me entranced. Help me narrow it down. If I had to decide I would have to say that my guess would be a piercing of some sort. Is that the correct half?

Now, remind me when are you traveling to visit your sisters?

I will look forward to possibly chatting with you.

More story?

D

February 24

Hello D,

We are going to go live this week on either Wednesday or Thursday early morning. It will be such a relief to have taken this step and once done, we can get to the job of fine tuning the data and reporting. I have a meeting w/ my president in two hours finalize this decision but I am confident this is the decision we will make.

And yes, you are close and correct on your guess for today. You're getting warmer....

I am going to Florida on the 21st of March and will be back sometime around the 26th or 27th. Then I am here for a week and go on vacation again the week of April 5. I still haven't decided what to do but that will come soon enough. I have to run for now; have yourself an awesome day!

~Miselena

February 25

Ah good morning Miselena,

And yes I hope it is a very good morning for you. Perhaps one that includes your company going live with its project. Good luck and "knock 'em dead".

I bet you could be knocked over with a feather when this is all done (relief).

Today's guess is perhaps a second or third piercing in your ear? Am I getting warmer or has my fantasy been realized and you nipples are pierced appropriately so that when I collar you, I can run a fine (thin) chain through your nipple loop as well?

As for your schedule, I learned today that there is a potential for me to have a one day meeting in Norfolk, VA sometime mid-March (perhaps the 18th). I thought our days might be close enough that we could have a bit of fun before you went down to show your sisters your surprise. If not for another meeting I would prolong my brief return to the states so that I could fly out to SD and give you a bit of stress relief but I am scheduled for another meeting in Lisbon, so I have to be out of VA by the 19th for a 20th meeting. I will see what I can work out. So as you see my life is racked with deadlines and meetings. You will be the source of my stress relief and our symbiotic pleasure will fuel our motivation to succeed in all things!

You have a great day and good luck! Chat tonight.

D.

February 25

Miselena: Hello D.

D: the piercing

Miselena: ha... yes... you're right

D: formal group, but the piercing says I will not be restrained by formal convention

D: nice

D: The more I learn the more I like

Miselena: well it is all about pushing my limits these days and I will not be afraid to do so anymore

D: Good

D: I did not think you would be afraid of pushing limits either

D: that is where I come in...

Miselena: well in the (recent) past I have allowed convention to rule a great many things

D: We will throw convention completely out the window!

Miselena: but this project at work has shown me that I can stretch

Miselena: yes... I am sure you will think outside the box

D: Oh I know we all are capable of a great many things

D: if only properly challenged

D: and motivated

Miselena: motivation has never been an issue for me...

D: somehow I believe that

D: Motivation or Enthusiasm

D: we will exploit both

Miselena: thank you... that was a lovely compliment

D: I am attempting to see what I can do with my schedule

D: did you get my email

Miselena: you will be in the states for a while; yes I did

D: Yes, potentially two days

Miselena: and when you come back to the states where will you land?

D: Are you talking about this time (potentially) or when I come back for good?

Miselena: for good

D: Oh San Diego!

D: That is no doubt

Miselena: ah ha.... I thought this was home for you

D: Yes

D: I noticed we have both taken a bit of time off from writing

D: although your story is much more intriguing

Miselena: yes... I have been working ridiculous hours

D: I can tell

D: I am very pleased we are able to chat tonight

Miselena: yes

D: Ok more tasks and you have to guess

D: The setting is the same backdrop you sent me from your apartment and private too

Miselena: but if it is private...

Miselena: that must mean windows?

D: You are good

Miselena: I am to display myself in my apartment with the windows open... may I hope it is daytime?

D: Damn you are very good

D: yes daytime

Miselena: ah... that is not so threatening

D: My dear I am not a threatening person

D: but how will you prove this?

Miselena: I have to say D, that my street is very busy

Miselena: for how long a period are we saying?

D: Not long at all, perhaps 5 minutes

Miselena: proving it is a piece of cake

Miselena: I have a digital camera

D: OHHHH

Miselena: so... I will send you a photo...

Miselena: you may count on deducting the full 15

D: I want a full 5 minutes

D: a picture a minute of your nude body during the day with your window as the frame

Miselena: consider it done...

D: Excellent

D: I am becoming extremely anxious for our first encounter my dear

Miselena: mmm

Miselena: I am beginning to wonder D...

D: wonder?

D: do not wonder nor worry

Miselena: how long have we been chatting now?

D: at this point it is inevitable

D: since about Nov?

Miselena: umm hmm... this started the day before my birthday in late October

Miselena: ah ha... you were a birthday present...

Miselena: lol

D: I will enjoy thoroughly exhausting you on several occasions

Miselena: mmm

D: If I can work the time for this meeting who knows maybe we will get to really tease each other

Miselena: when are you thinking?

D: next week

Miselena: hmm.. I'll keep it free for now

D: Good, I'll see what I can do...

Miselena: that's mid week so it will have to be in the evening

D: I agree...

Miselena: k

Miselena: mmm...

D: it excites me to think of you in the ways we will play

Miselena: I fantasize too

Miselena: this is a first and vanilla meeting isn't it?

D: yes

Miselena: I remember now...

D: it will be the first and LAST vanilla meeting we will have if we are satisfied with the first

D: after that the limits begin to shed like layers of clothing

Miselena: I am getting warm...

D: very, very good

D: have you had a bit of wine Miselena?

Miselena: about a half glass

D: mmmmm

D: very nice

D: it is good that you are relaxed

Miselena: ha...

Miselena: I don't think so...

D: I know you are still going live tonight

Miselena: I have that kind of nervous exhaustion going on that makes your body feel like it is buzzing... do you know what I mean?... with a knot in your stomach

D: so tell me Miselena,

Miselena: yes...

D: will you be truly relieved when this is done tonight?

Miselena: yes...

Miselena: oh yes

D: Do you enjoy my stories?

Miselena: yes I love your stories

D: good

D: then we will give each other more to reflect on later in life

D: what are you wearing Miselena

Miselena: flannel pajama pants and a crop top

D: hmmm that navel ring would should look sexy with a crop top

D: have you ever fantasized about being fondled in a crowd, perhaps in a mini skirt with no panties standing so close together

Miselena: um... no... can't say I have

D: and then feeling someone touching you,

D: your first thought is to scream

D: you look around but can't tell who it is

D: it continues

D: embarrassed by how wet and excited you are getting

D: as some stranger presses against your body

D: surrounded by well dressed men AND women

D: not knowing

D: completely silent

D: as someone gently caresses your vagina

D: feeling your legs open

D: naturally

D: to provide them greater access

D: to your sex

D: unaware of who would be so bold

D: searching around you for a hint

D: but catching no ones eye

D: you look around and a very handsome gentleman winks

D: with a gentle smile

D: well dressed

D: clean cut

D: would you scream?

Miselena: no

Miselena: I'm the behind the scenes, low profile type

Miselena: I would turn around and wait for him to speak (with a question on my face...)

Miselena: but I could imagine Ahsan setting something like that up and warning Lisa to expect it...

D: He continues to finger your vagina, running the tips of his fingers over your lips

D: Yes Miselena I would set something like this up..

D: perhaps it would not be me, performing the action

D: but watching your reaction

Miselena: no... I expect not

D: and enjoying the conflict within you

D: setting this up, with a trusted friend

D: telling him to seek you out

D: and the only instructions I would give you is where to be, and to ensure you were without panties

D: you would suspect me, but the uncertainty would only increase your excitement

D: I can see you now looking around for me

D: but I am out of sight

D: and the probing continues

D: you try to contain yourself, your heart is throbbing

D: the intensity of the throbbing between your legs grows

D: your clit is now swollen

D: and your breath short and shallow

D: you do not want to draw attention to what is going on below your waist

D: you do not want it to stop

D: your legs begin to shake

D: standing there

D: and as you relax you feel the gentle probing of a finger teasing the entrance to your ass

D: it almost makes you jump in place

D: surprised

D: you relax

D: and settle gently onto the finger that is probing

D: your mouth opens and you reach into your purse for a set of dark shades

D: so that you can close your eyes and enjoy the feelings that have taken over your senses

D: you are surprised that your body has so easily accepted this stimulation

D: you would have never guessed that you would be so excited

D: so close to orgasm

D: surrounded by so many people

D: your labia are now swollen

D: and you fear that the juice that flows from you will be seen once the area clears

D: will there be remnants, evidence of what has occurred

D: for the moment you are lost in the stimulating fingers that have penetrated your anus and continue to brush your clit

D: bodies

D: so

D: close

D: so warm

D: pressed so hard against you

D: could you cum?

Miselena: mmm... I don't know...

D: Touch your clitoris Miselena

D: and tell me are you excited

Miselena: very

D: squeeze your clit my pet

D: firmly

D: and think of the bodies pressed against your skin

D: the crowd

D: so many different scents

D: so many people surrounding you

D: and you are so exposed

D: your vagina

D: open

D: dripping

D: begging

D: yet you know

D: this is so taboo

D: so completely taboo

D: someone fingering your anus

D: gently brush your clitoris for me

D: and massage your labia

D: opening them for me

D: I would have my partner whisper in your ear,

D: Your master is pleased

D: a complete stranger

D: probing your intimate desires

D: feeling you in ways that are reserved for the most intimate settings

D: your cell phone rings and it is me

D: Miselena very, very good

D: I am so pleased with you my pet

D: You instinctively search the crowd for me

D: I halt that action

D: do not look for me

D: or our game will stop

D: are you enjoying my friend

D: and you answer yes

D: in almost a whisper

D: She is very good isn't she?

D: and I can see the surprise in your face

D: just kidding my pet

D: today my pleasure for you is a man

D: Miselena I want you to press your nipples between your fingers

D: now

D: press them hard for me

D: I want you to feel the pressure that borders on pain

D: pull your nipples away from your body

D: extending your breast out

D: exaggerating the size of your breast

D: now massage your breast

D: kneed them

D: massaging them with the palms of your hands

D: now run your hand down your stomach slowly tracing the lines to your navel, then your vagina

D: run your fingers to your pubic mound and gently circle your clitoris as if your fingers were a gentle feather

D: now massage your vagina

D: oh yes Miselena

D: very good

D: deeper

D: harder

D: massage your sex until your labia open

D: remove your pants and spread your legs wide

D: Now picture my tongue running the length of your sex

D: from your ass to the tip of your swollen clitoris

D: flicking my tongue

D: tasting you

D: sucking your clit as if I were performing fellatio on you

D: taking you into my mouth

D: and gently pulling your clit

D: circling my tongue around the hood of your clitoris

D: then tasting your sex

D: put a finger inside your vagina

D: deep

D: now two

D: spread your vagina open

D: prepare for me my dear

D: now remove your fingers and run them softly

D: over your lips

D: softly over your lips

D: like a gentle kiss

D: like a gentle kiss from me

D: after I've tasted your sex

D: run your finger softly over your lips opening them slightly

D: then inserting them into your mouth

D: I want to taste you like that

D: then share your sexual juices in a passionate kiss

D: remove your fingers and caress your vagina

D: are you wet for me?

Miselena: yes

D: Good

D: I will stretch you Miselena

D: in so many ways

D: anal

D: vaginal

D: I will take you into safe places and demand your obedience

D: completely discreet

D: completely mine

D: you will be rocked by orgasm

D: even at the hands of others

D: open your ass Miselena

D: and think of me inspecting what is yours to give

D: relax

D: and imagine

D: my fingers probing your ass

D: lubricating you for what is to come

D: sliding so effortlessly into your ass

D: applying a great amount of lubrication for our pleasure

D: and our play

D: and while I slide my fingers into your ass

D: I take your sex into my mouth

D: spreading you open with my tongue

D: penetrating you with my tongue as if to fuck you with it

D: you are so wet and taste so good to me

D: I want to stay there

D: but not at the expense of your orgasm

D: not yet

D: I lift my head just short of your climax

D: your anus so well lubricated and relaxed

D: I find that two fingers slide easily inside

D: now three and I feel you lift gently your ass being stretched

D: I return to provide the oral pleasure that we both enjoy

D: your legs spread wider than I've ever seen them

D: and I feel your anus relaxing under my tender probe

D: You want to release and let go

D: but not yet

D: I have more for you...

D: I brought my large phallus

D: and tonight you will take it anally

D: You fear you can not

D: but we are slow and gentle

D: I begin with more oral pleasure spreading your vagina

D: so delicately your entire body relaxes under my oral stimulation

D: your head rolled back

D: your mouth open

D: your juice flowing into my mouth

D: so sweet to me

D: I begin by probing the entrance to you anus

D: slowly very, very slowly

D: continuing with my lips massaging your vagina, circling your lips as if I am locked in the most passionate French kiss

D: your ass so relaxed and open

D: My toy probing delicately

D: the tip is in....

D: put a finger in your ass now!

D: slowly you feel your anus spreading open,

D: I am continuing to lick and suck your genitals

D: while inserting this massive toy deeper and deeper

D: you are surprised that you have taken so much

D: and I lift my head but for a brief second to acknowledge my pleasure and appreciation,

D: You are giving yourself completely

D: and releasing all that is not pleasing to us

D: letting go

D: deeper and deeper

D: You feel stretched to the limit and unable to take anymore

D: put another finger in your ass!

D: but I continue and you receive our toy little by little

D: You are surprised by your tolerance and capability

D: but I am not

D: It is full inside you, and you feel stretched like no other time in your life

D: three fingers in your ass now!

D: it borders on pain but the pressure provides such pleasurable stimulation

D: I lift to say Miselena my pet, you have been pleasing to me tonight and you may cum

D: with that I run my tongue over your vagina

D: as if to devour

D: your sex into my mouth

D: opening you up

D: sucking

D: licking

D: penetrating you

D: taking all your liquid into my mouth

D: and flicking my tongue over your labia, clit and vulva

D: you may cum

D: massage your vagina for me my pet

D: massage it as if my mouth were covering your sex

D: drinking your juice and sharing your pleasure

D: massage your wet vagina and think of me

D: deep inside your ass!

Miselena: ah... D... now I'm relaxed...

Miselena: ha.. I have to tell you something...

D: sure...

Miselena: I bought myself a toy...

D: very good

Miselena: shall I make you guess?

D: ha...

Miselena: if you cannot guess correctly in 10 guesses I get 5 more taken off... lol

D: LOL....

D: Ok

D: Rubber, Vibrator?

Miselena: no...one

D: ha,ha,ha...

D: Nipple clamp?

Miselena: two

D: ha-ha,...

D: Is it an adult toy?

Miselena: yes

D: clit clamp?

Miselena: three

D: butt plug?

Miselena: four

D: Ben Wa Balls

Miselena: ahh...

Miselena: very good

D: Wow... that is awesome

D: did you play with them tonight?

Miselena: no

D: have you played with them yet?

Miselena: yes... I rather like them and fantasize about anal sex when I use them

Miselena: I think that combination could be good...

D: Sometimes they have strings attached sometimes they are just balls which do you have?

Miselena: no strings

D: mmmmmm

Miselena: that will undoubtedly go in a story somewhere... lol

D: where do you put them? vagina?

Miselena: yes

D: awesome

Miselena: they are very... I don't know what the word is...but I like them

D: Now I have something have you ever walked with them inside

Miselena: no

D: You are right they will go in a story

D: Tell me what excited you about them or why were they your choice?

Miselena: I came across them at a vendor's booth in the flea market

D: My pet you have unbounded potential

D: ha,ha,ha

D: that is great,

D: I think you may surprise yourself when we begin to play

Miselena: hmmm

Miselena: I may

D: It will be interesting when you display yourself to me for the first time.

Miselena: yes I agree

D: and

D: masturbate

Miselena: ah ha... that too

D: soon now

D: Are you truly a bit more relaxed now?

Miselena: yes

Miselena: and tired

Miselena: I'm fading

D: I was just getting ready to say you must be exhausted and I know you have to get up

D: soooo

D: I enjoyed tonight's chat...

Miselena: yes, me too... I'm glad we connected

D: don't forget my payment with the window frame...

D: can't wait to see you in the flesh.

Miselena: have an awesome day... I will get to it

D: Good night my pet...

Miselena: nite

***

February 28

Hello D

Have I told you lately how much I love our chats? Even now I'm throbbing with remembrance and anticipation. Soon really is soon now isn't it?

~Miselena

February 28

Prepare yourself Miselena for you are about to be tested,

Everything we have discussed, suggested, longed for is about to begin. This Saturday dress in a blouse that buttons up the front and a skirt that is full enough for you to open your legs. Make it casual; wear open sandals. Do not wear panties or a bra. Be ready by 10:00 am and plan on being gone the entire day. If we agree after our coffee we will want the time.

I will see you soon, assess you soon and test you soon. I will touch you in ways you have only imagined up to now. I will make you want; make you need and make you shudder in release.

You will do as I say, offer yourself freely and open yourself up to me. You will decide what happens next, if we take the next step; the one that leads to your freedom.

Should you choose yes you may expect to be tested immediately. Your full and prompt compliance is the only acceptable response. I say this now to ensure you fully understand each instance of disobedience will result in compensation and the only way to stop once this day is started is to play your safe word ending it completely. Are you ready?

www.ingramcontent.com/pod-product-compliance
Lightning Source LLC
Chambersburg PA
CBHW030156070426
42447CB00031B/498